READ ON

Using Fiction in the Primary School

STUART MARRIOTT

P·C·P

Paul Chapman
Publishing Ltd

Paul Chapman Publishing Ltd
144 Liverpool Road
London
N1 1LA

British Library Cataloguing in Publication Data

Marriott, Stuart
  Read on: Using Fiction in the Primary
  School
  I. Title
  372.4

  ISBN 1–85396–286–4

Typeset by Anneset, Weston-super-Mare, Avon
Printed and bound by The Baskerville Press, Salisbury, Wiltshire

A B C D E F G H 9 8 7 6 5

Contents

Introduction

It is from the conviction that hearing and reading stories is vital for children, all children, that this book has been written. The experience of stories has immense benefits in terms of children's reading development, but in addition it also provides them with access to a limitless world of artistry and imagination and to vicarious experience infinitely more extensive and complex than the ordinary reality of home and school.

It is not usually children in general who first come to mind when we think of the interaction of readers with stories but individuals: particular children reading specific texts in unique contexts. So before beginning the lengthy and serious business of evaluating the educational role of fiction in detail, a discussion which is necessarily to some extent rather broad and general, one or two examples of the everyday encounters of children with stories may be worth while; it is the quality of such individual experience, and that of all the similar but different children who no doubt spring into the reader's mind, that makes the topic worth consideration.

> Gerard, aged ten, is a very able boy. His teacher tells him that since he is such a good reader he ought to try *The Lord of the Rings*, because, she says jokingly, it's the longest book in the world. A few weeks later Gerard brings a battered copy into the classroom, his face lit up with pride in his achievement.

> Mary, aged fourteen, and severely handicapped, is immersed in Jan Ormerod's wordless picture book *Sunshine*. She refuses to give the book back to her teacher at the end of school, and takes it home with her. Next day, her mother reports that Mary held tight all evening, took the book to bed with her, and as yet will still not let go.

> On a warm summer's day in Belfast, a group of eight-year-olds are sitting on the wall outside the public library listening to the librarian read a story. An

army truck drives by. In spite of the librarian's efforts to restrain them, the children rush towards the road, hurling a few stones and plenty of abuse as the truck disappears round the corner. The children return, sit down quietly, and are soon absorbed in *The Great Piratical Rumbustification* once again.

Kevin, aged eleven, finds reading very difficult. 'Not to worry', says his Dad, 'I can't read either, and I'm not short of a bob or two'.

Miss Hammond is reading the last chapters of *The Turbulent Term of Tyke Tiler* to her class. There is a stunned silence as the amazing truth about Tyke sinks in. Several children deny that it is possible, because a girl just wouldn't make friends with someone like Danny. But Victoria says that a boy just the same as Danny lives next door to her, and she's his friend.

Each of these brief sketches has a wide variety of implications, but at least they illustrate a few of the circumstances in which stories can attract and engross young people. They hint, too, at the inherent flexibility of fiction, the prodigious variety of contexts in which readers can engage with texts, the potential of stories to have real and powerful – if often unpredictable – effects, and the ways in which they may extend and deepen children's insights into their own and others' experience.

For classroom teachers, of course, all this may be true, but it is not yet enough. For them, the role that stories play in improving and enlarging children's understanding of the way language works, and in enhancing their accuracy and fluency in reading and writing is very significant. This role is important at all ages and stages of education, but particularly at Key Stage 2 in the primary school, because this is a crucial period in the development of readers and readership. It is between the ages of 7 and 11, or thereabouts, that children can become skilful and committed readers like Gerard, with enormous benefits both at the time and in later life, or conversely like Kevin, for any one of a great variety of reasons, fail to make progress and sooner or later decide that this reading business is really not for them.

While the early stages of learning to read are vital, the later primary school years are thus just as crucial in developing and extending the quantity and quality of children's cognitive, emotional and especially literary experience through what and how they read. For this reason, although this book may be of interest and value to teachers of children of all ages, it is mainly focused on the middle and upper primary school.

The purpose of the book is to provide, in a relatively concise form, both a rationale and a strategy for the use of fiction in the central years of school. Much of the discussion is of obvious relevance to children's reading development, but the focus is broader than techniques and methods of teaching reading: first and foremost it is on the ways in which readers and stories can be productively engaged. In Chapter 1, therefore, the value of books in general and fiction in particular is briefly considered, before exploring the effects of the interaction of readers and texts in terms of the personal, social, intellectual and curricular implications of stories. In Chapter 2 the prescriptions and advice of the National Curriculum concerning ways in which children's fiction should be used are described, and some of the evidence relating to actual practice in schools is assessed. Chapter 3 provides an outline of a policy framework for the use of fiction in the upper primary school, discussing in particular how books and other resources can be organized and most effectively made available to children. In Chapter 4 the appropriate use of fiction in the teaching and learning activities of the classroom is considered, especially the question of how readers and books can best be matched. Chapter 5 focuses on ideas about how readers read and respond to texts and some of the consequent implications for work with children, and in Chapter 6 a variety of practical ideas are suggested for the use of some specific books in the classroom.

The hero of *Bill's New Frock*, after a day of being treated as a girl, yells: 'I am a *person*!' While I have mostly used 'she' for the teacher and sometimes 'he' for a pupil, this is merely for convenience and no other motives should be inferred.

ACKNOWLEDGEMENTS

I am grateful to Harold Brownlow, Trina Donaghy, and my colleagues Gordon Rae and Michael O'Hara for their help with this book at various times and in various ways. Particular thanks to Lesley also, for help with this and much else. And as my son Aidan's comment – 'Oh no you're not writing another *ghastly* book' – suggests, thanks to him and to Nicholas for their steadfast refusal to be impressed.

CHILDREN'S BOOKS

FINE, ANNE, *Bill's New Frock*, Puffin.
KEMP, GENE, *The Turbulent Term of Tyke Tiler*, Puffin.

Read On

MAHY, MARGARET, *The Great Piratical Rumbustification*, Puffin.
ORMEROD, JAN, *Sunshine*, Puffin.
TOLKIEN, J. R. R., *The Lord of the Rings*, Allen & Unwin.

1
The Value of Fiction

I am writing this on the keyboard of a personal computer. As I write, the words appear on a screen in front of me. I am using a desktop publishing package which, among other things, enables me to insert, delete and move chunks of text around within my document instantaneously by pressing a few keys. Then, when I am satisfied with what I have written so far, I can save my work on to a small disk and return to it another time, or if I wish I can print it out on paper; the machine even beeps at me if I make a spelling or typing mistake. Nothing particularly surprising in all this, of course, because there must be millions of people now who spend at least part of their working lives using computers in this way, and such machines are now taken-for-granted aspects of our society. But if I had been writing this ten or eleven years ago I would have been using my brand-new, gleaming electric typewriter. I thought it was wonderful: no need to whack at the keys, it just needed a feather-light touch. I still had to struggle with carbon paper and correcting fluid, of course, and if I wanted to edit the text it needed scissors and glue, but nevertheless it was a vast improvement on drafting in ball-point pen and then trying to find someone who could be bribed into typing it out for me.

But my computer is slightly different from those commonly used in offices and shops; if I get bored with writing I can press a few different keys and immerse myself in a game of chess, playing against the computer – I always lose, it's far too good for me. Or if I feel like something less intellectually demanding I can play an arcade game, shooting up baddies, rescuing damsels in distress, fighting aliens from outer space, or even saving the universe from destruction. Again, nothing particularly unusual about this: computer games are now found in millions of homes. But it's only ten or a dozen years since I bought my first colour television. I thought it was brilliant: nature programmes, sport, drama all came alive as they never did on my grainy old black and white.

5

The point is obvious, of course: in Western industrialized societies techno-logical change has touched almost every aspect of the way we live. It has changed the nature of work for many and it has transformed leisure for almost all of us. Indeed, it could be argued that at least since the early years of this century, and probably long before, our society has been fundamentally shaped by the emergence of more and more sophisticated technological innovations which have competed for a share of audiences and markets. In particular, the variety and accessibility of our means of entertainment have vastly increased: from radio and cinema sixty years ago, through television and tape recorders in the post-war years, to videos, computer games and compact discs in the last decade. At the same time, generally increasing affluence, partly itself dependent on technological change, has made this electronic culture available to the majority in a way which was not the case in earlier times.

Furthermore, the pace at which such changes occur is increasing all the time. Thousands of years of civilization were needed before the printing press partly replaced the pen, hundreds more for the typewriter to appear, but only a further few decades for the electric typewriter and then the first relatively primitive computer systems to arrive, to be replaced in turn only a few years later by my extraordinarily sophisticated desktop publishing package. The same acceleration of technological change can be traced in the development of recording of sound and images: the pace of development has escalated from the earliest cameras and sound recordings through to the introduction of video, teletext, car telephones, and hand-held computer games. And if there is one thing that is certain it is that in a few more years there will be some new micro-electronic wizardry – virtual reality? artificial intelligence? robotics? – at first to astound us and very soon after to be taken for granted among all the other gadgets with which we surround ourselves.

In such a world, the world in which our children will live, what place will there be for reading and for books? As far into the future as it is possible to see it's surely certain that literacy will remain essential; wherever words appear, they have to be read, understood and acted on. But what of the specific physical forms of books and magazines and newspapers? While technological developments have obviously touched the publishing industry through the introduction of paperbacks, photographic reproduction, colour printing, and so on, books remain recognizably the same objects as they were a hundred or more years ago. Will they gradually now begin to fade away in the face of technological change, or will there always be a substantial, if not, perhaps, pre-eminent role for the book? Will the physical object of paper and ink be replaced, or transformed into 'words which dance in light'?[1] Will the purposes to which reading is put change? Will it be seen increasingly as a functional matter, necessary for work, for education, for coping with the demands of everyday life, but more and more replaced by the video and the CD rom for entertainment? Or, alternatively, will easy access to vast quantities of information in gigantic databases be accompanied by a renewed emphasis on written stories as a source of aesthetic pleasure?

There are plenty more questions where these ones come from, and precious few definitive answers, I suspect. But while some of the characteristics of books may be increasingly emulated by tapes, videos, disks and other wonders, there remain good reasons to think that books will continue to be published and read. Books do not really compete with audio-visual or electronic media but complement them; just as radio can coexist with television, photography with painting, cinema with video, so in principle at least there will remain an important place for the written word. And thus books, whether or not in their present physical form, will probably continue to be required and continue to be used.

If this is true in general terms, some more questions arise in relation to the specific form of fiction and its effects and functions. For example, what needs do stories meet? How does fiction work, and what do readers do with it? How do readers interact with texts? What reasons are there for suggesting that fiction is of such value that it will endure in a world in which, it seems, everything else is changing so rapidly? Further questions of particular relevance to the teacher also need to be considered. What functions does fiction fulfil for children? What is the relationship between reading stories and children's developing competences in language and literacy? And are stories so important that at a time when the curriculum is full to bursting they should retain a significant place in the work of primary schools?

None of these questions is easy to answer, and indeed whole books have been devoted to each of them. But even though a full discussion is well beyond the scope of this chapter, it is worth looking briefly at some of the reasons why stories are of value, especially for children, because such an account is needed to provide a context and a rationale for the use of fiction in the classroom. First, therefore, a summary of reasons and justifications for the use of fiction may be helpful, under four broad headings relating to the personal, social, intellectual and curricular dimensions of stories.

Personal

Fiction can and does have a variety of effects and implications for the individual reader. A very simple but very important reason for reading stories needs to be first.

FICTION IS ENJOYABLE

One of the main reasons why we, children or adults, read fiction is because stories are enjoyable. Fiction can offer pleasure and relaxation, can make us laugh or cry, can provoke or console us. Stories can take us away from the dull routines of our everyday world, can enable us to dream, to fantasize, to make believe; they can allow us to escape to a more dramatic, colourful or congenial world in which we can be rich, powerful, famous, intelligent or beautiful. For most readers, then, and especially children, the expectation of fun and pleasure is very often why we start a story with anticipation and continue to read eagerly.

Most of the more gloomy forecasts of the future of fiction[2] see the ability of audio-visual technologies to provide instant, visually attractive and undemanding entertainment as undermining this role of books. Indeed, every few years there seems to be a period of public dismay at allegations that children have totally forsaken reading for, in the current case, computer games. A year or two ago it was videos, and I am just old enough to remember the intense and worried debates of the early 1950s when, it was feared, the emergence of television as a mass medium would lead to the terminal decline of reading and the emergence of generations of illiterate and passive viewers. Although the wilder of these claims can be discounted, it may well be that television and other technologies have to some extent taken and will increasingly take over the entertainment role of light fiction. But by no means entirely: for many children and adults the book is likely to retain a significant place in leisure activities, and there is also some evidence that television viewing can stimulate fiction reading.[3]

One of the reasons why books will continue to be used for simple escapist pleasure, prosaic as it may seem, is because they are so convenient and accessible. As Landsberg has put it, books are valuable for, and valued by, children partly because: 'They can be hugged, chewed, carried to bed or to a secret hideout in a tree, read and re-read, and the reader is always in control – skipping, going back, absorbing deeply or skimming forward.'[4] Books are and will probably remain relatively cheap, plentiful, portable, easily available, accessible and user-friendly. Books can be read anywhere, any time, and they don't need electrical sockets or batteries or cables or equipment of any kind. Books are robust and will survive being dropped and trodden on, kicked around the classroom floor, or even being left out in the rain. (A little girl I once knew decided, for her own mysterious purposes, to bury a favourite book in the garden, wrapped up in a plastic bag. When some months later for equally inscrutable reasons she dug it up again it had survived the ordeal and regained its normal place on her bookshelf.)

If the pleasures of reading consisted only of providing a form of relatively superficial light entertainment the future of the written story might be doubtful, but there is obviously more to it than that. While sometimes we may read simply for relaxation and escape, at other times we read for more sophisticated pleasures. For example, we may read to appreciate the quality of the writing or a distinctive and attractive style, or we may enjoy a subtle and intriguing story or skilful characterization. At such times the story engages more of our intellect and we have to work a bit harder in order to get the most from it. As we learn to read better, then, we gradually realize that stories may not always be immediately attractive and exciting, but nevertheless it is often worth while persevering. Sometimes we enjoy a story even more if we have had to work a little harder at it.

The main point, however, is clear. Unless we, as adult or child readers, find the experience of reading stories at some level fulfilling and enjoyable, the other beneficial effects of reading fiction are unlikely to occur, because most of us tend in the end to give up experiences which are not in some way rewarding. As teachers, therefore, the pleasure of reading needs to be at the front of our minds constantly when we are thinking about the significance of fiction for classroom work.

It's worth noting here, briefly, an obvious but often forgotten point which is of particular importance to the role of the teacher. Readers are individuals and respond to books in personal and sometimes eccentric ways; indeed, part of the enjoyment of reading fiction is the fact that we do have different opinions of stories which we can discuss or even argue about with other people. Sometimes, for example, we value a book which to others has no apparent literary or aesthetic merit because it was read at an especially significant time in our lives, or in a place with especially powerful associations. Such highly idiosyncratic responses are by their nature impossible to legislate for or categorize, yet for many readers, again often including children,[5] they provide powerful reasons for valuing a particular book, which should not be neglected when it comes to choosing books for children to read.

FICTION CONTRIBUTES TO PERSONAL GROWTH

This is a complex set of reasons for valuing fiction, ones which are quite difficult to pin down, concerning the ways in which stories affect or interact with the person reading.

It has often been asserted that literature's most important effects are much more complex than relatively trivial entertainment, that fiction can enlarge the imagination and develop the personality of the reader in ways that television can rarely if ever achieve. In the words of the Bullock Committee nearly twenty years ago, much has been claimed for the role of literature in this area: 'that it helps to shape the personality, refine the sensibility, sharpen the critical intelligence; that it is a powerful instrument for empathy, a medium through which the child can acquire his values.'[6] As the Bullock Committee also noted, however, such claims are easier to make than to substantiate. In particular, the idea that literature has positive effects on the reader's moral values is very difficult to demonstrate. It is of course possible that reading a story may have a morally uplifting effect, but it is equally true that some of the most unpleasant characters in history have been very well read.

It seems more likely that one of the ways in which fiction affects us is that we can compare ourselves – our ideas, our decisions, our thinking, our feeling – with that of others. By vicariously participating in a story, we can become aware of possibilities and intentions and motives that we had never thought of before; these may confirm the image we have of ourselves, our sense of self, our choices and decisions and opinions, or it may in some respects change it. For a young reader, especially, whose ideas and personality are not yet fully developed, a story can help to build or reinforce understanding of the kind of person he or she is. A simple example is provided by a group of four 10-year-old girls reading part of Sheila Lavelle's *My Best Fiend* together.[7] In the story, pheasants are bred and released in order to be shot, which prompts a discussion of killing animals and of occupations in which such killing is a requirement:

PAULINE: I don't think it's really fair.
GILLIAN: No it isn't 'cause if I saw something like that really happen I'd hate to be in a job like gamekeeper or the RSPCA.

ALICE: Yeah they just have to put animals down.

PAULINE: My aunt got her dog put down the other week.

GILLIAN: My dad's second cousin got his hamster put down 'cause you see it had the flu.

Very often in such discussions children will express their feelings almost entirely through anecdotes from their own experience relating to the theme, but on this occasion this is preceded by more general comments which suggest that the girls are currently uncertain – and not entirely consistent – about a sensitive issue, but that a collective view is emerging that certain occupations are inherently distasteful. A rather different kind of example is provided by Donald Fry in his fascinating account of children as developing readers. He describes how Clayton, aged 8, uses his reading to develop and sustain his sense of himself as an expert on farming, like his father:

> Clayton's status as someone who knows about farming is supported by the books, pamphlets, brochures and magazines that he collects. They help him, too, to be like his father, but also an authority in his own right. *Watership Down* gives him a similar opportunity to establish an expertise: in that respect his move into fiction is an extension of what he already values in information books, especially as he makes it in the company of his father.[8]

In such ways, then, the reader's response to literature may in part consist of an affirmation or reaffirmation of some aspect of personal image; he may define himself in relation to the stories he reads. As Applebee has argued, stories work in this way by: 'presenting alternatives, clarifying dark corners, posing contradictions, reconciling conflicts within the realm of our subjective, personal experience'.[9] Or, to put it more simply, fiction can help the reader to answer Alice's question in Wonderland: '"Who in the world am I?" Ah, that's the great puzzle!'.

FICTION PROMOTES EMPATHY

Stories contribute to children's learning in further subtle ways too. By exploring stories the reader can compare his or her own experience with the real or imagined experience of others. By beginning to understand the motives and decisions that characters in stories make, the reader can to a greater extent make sense of and come to terms with the real world.

Although few of us are ever likely to be in the predicament that faces King Lear in the storm, or in the position of the assassin in *The Day of the Jackal* as he peers at President De Gaulle through his telescopic sights, or for that matter encounter at first hand the problems of Wilbur – the pig who will soon become sliced bacon unless Charlotte the spider can help him – in *Charlotte's Web*, the experience of reading such stories provides insights into and points of comparison and contrast with our own experience, how it is and how it might be. Thus, the young reader does not just know more about evacuation in wartime having read *Goodnight Mr Tom*, or about travelling people by reading *The Diddakoi*, or of the famine in Ireland by reading *Under the Hawthorn Tree* (although he or she certainly does know more) but he or she is also enabled to feel what it is like and enter into the experience. For example, an extended discussion of Beverly Cleary's *Dear Mr Henshaw* enables the same group of girls quoted earlier to feel quite powerfully engaged by the ending of the story:

ALICE: Another part I liked where – his mother and father sat down and had a cup of tea.

GILLIAN: That was near the end.

ALICE: I felt inside me that it must have been the first time in years that they had tea together – in the same room.

BEVERLEY: And they were sitting together and then they both hugged each other.

PAULINE: I thought they were going to get back together again.
(*Chorus of agreement*)

GILLIAN: Pity 'cause I was enjoying that.

ALICE: I suppose all stories don't have happy endings.

GILLIAN: Oh, that was a kind of happy ending, but I half cried.
(*Chorus of agreement*)

ALICE: I couldn't read any more and I was on page hundred and thirteen.

PAULINE: I wanted to read more, I wanted more.

GILLIAN: I wanted to read until his father and mother met up – until they got married again.

Similarly, I recently read Martin Waddell and Philippe Dupasquier's *Going West* with a group of 8-year-olds. It's an exciting story of a pioneer family encountering all sorts of peril as they travel across America to find a new home. The children were gripped by and enthusiastic about the adventure and Philippe Dupasquier's panoramic illustrations until the point at which the child narrator's little sister dies from illness. The text says: 'There was a blizzard. The snow stopped us. Louisa died.' As I read these words the children were absolutely silent for several moments as, I think, they began to consider what such a death might mean, and to relate it to their own possible experiences and feelings. I cannot be sure, but I felt at the time that the story had touched the children in a very powerful way.

Reading stories can in a similar way help children to begin to understand and face the real problems that they sometimes experience. A lonely child may at least discover through stories that his feelings are not unique, or a child, where family relationships are difficult, may be helped by a story in which family conflict is resolved. Direct and powerful effects of these kinds may be unusual although they do occur, but fiction may also clarify and illuminate familiar and everyday events and problems like going to the doctor, being told off by your teacher, fear of the dark, and so on. To quote from a discussion of Oralee Wachter's *No More Secrets for Me*, which consists of stories centred on the theme of helping children to avoid abuse, at one point the same four girls begin to consider the implications of the book for the nature of secrets and what and whom one should tell:

ALICE: It tells you that sometimes if you tell somebody a secret it can really help.

GILLIAN: Yes, if you tell somebody something that you don't like.

PAULINE: I always share all my secrets with Alice and Beverley –

GILLIAN: And me. I shared a secret with all of you.

ALICE: Should you keep it to yourself?

GILLIAN: Some secrets just shouldn't be kept.

Of course, this is not to suggest that any problem in real life can be easily solved by reading a story about it – the principles of what has been called bibliotherapy seem rather dubious to me – but rather that fiction can sometimes play a part in demystifying such experience, and by increasing the reader's self-awareness enable him to come to terms with it.

While this ability of stories to create empathy is often apparent in stories which are based on or connected with the real world, the same is also true of stories set in imaginary worlds of fantasy. In fact, it is often the case that even though the context and the plot may be very distant from here and now, or even utterly bizarre, the feelings, motives and relationships of the characters are exposed even more sharply than usual. Fantasy, therefore, whether for children (like *The Borrowers* or *A Wizard of Earthsea*) or for adults

(*Gulliver's Travels*) often has as much to say about real human experience as stories set in the everyday world.

For all these reasons reading fiction may have direct effects on the reader's own experience, sometimes in relatively trivial but occasionally in profound ways. In the second report of the Cox Committee on the teaching of English, the potential of literature to have a variety of personal effects on children are neatly summarized: 'An active involvement with literature enables pupils to share the experience of others. They will encounter and come to understand a wide range of feelings and relationships by entering vicariously the worlds of others, and in consequence they are likely to understand more of themselves.'[10] Such implications of literature for the reader's personality, feelings, perceptions and relationships are for many the most important effects of fiction, but clearly there are several other significant issues.

Social

The term social is meant to indicate the ways in which fiction can extend experience of the physical and social world beyond the immediate constraints of the here and now.

FICTION PROVIDES ACCESS TO CULTURAL HERITAGE

Stories permeate our society in profound ways. That the stories of the Bible, Shakespeare, and Dickens are part of our culture, part of the meanings and understandings shared by most speakers and readers of English, is obvious. But *Cinderella* and *Baa Baa Black Sheep* are also part of the cultural heritage of many of us, as are *Alice in Wonderland* and *The Lion, the Witch and the Wardrobe*. Rather less obviously, perhaps, *The Secret Diary of Adrian Mole*, *Dan Dare*, *The Bash Street Kids*, and many other similar examples of popular literature have powerful implications. Our minds are full of stories because we live in a society in which written stories have a fundamental place and 'we are what we eat, we are told, and we are – at least in part – what we have read'.[11] One of the ways this becomes obvious is in our everyday talk, which is full of references to stories, even if we are not always conscious of the original source of what we are saying: a man is described as a Romeo (Shakespeare) or as being 'hard as nails' (Dickens), a puzzling event is 'curiouser and curiouser' (Carroll), a child is 'crying wolf', or disappointment leads to 'sour grapes' (Aesop). Our understanding of the society in which we live, then, is partly constructed by our awareness of its cultural heritage, which to a large extent comprises the writings of generations of tellers of stories.

It's also worth noting at this point that many readers in a society as diverse and plural as ours are heirs to the cultural traditions of the Caribbean, of the Indian subcontinent, or elsewhere; for these readers the stories of *Anansi* or *Prince Rama* or *Finn Mac Cool* may have an especially compelling resonance. While the principle of cultural heritage remains constant, it can thus take a variety of forms, and it provides an agenda for readers – including children – in the mutual exploration of the different social roots of our experience.

FICTION WIDENS EXPERIENCE

By taking what has been called the 'spectator' role, stories can enable the reader to explore experience as if from the inside, in ways which would otherwise be difficult if not impossible. Our firsthand experience is necessarily limited by the accidents of birth, upbringing, geography and history, yet one of our characteristics as human beings is the ability to go beyond the constraints of the here and the now and learn from real or imagined experience mediated through images or words. One of the most important ways this can happen is through stories; indeed one definition of fiction could be the description of possible experiences. For all readers – especially children, whose firsthand experience is even more limited than that of adults – stories enable us to broaden our minds and extend our horizons by introducing us to people, places and situations we could otherwise never encounter.

So important is fiction in this representation of experience that, for example, much of the general knowledge of educated adults is acquired in this way rather than at first hand or through other sources: what we know about the lives and works of the kings of England may well be largely derived from the works of Shakespeare, and our knowledge of everyday life in times past often relies more on the novels of Austen, Hardy and Dickens than on the work of any academic historian. And so in similar ways can children acquire information and learn more about the physical and social world through stories. For example, a skilfully written story about life in eighteenth-century London (like *Smith*) or in Roman Britain (*The Eagle of the Ninth*) can help children to make some sense of a period which otherwise seems impossibly remote from everyday experience. In the same way a novel located in another country can illustrate the myriad different forms of social life that are possible (such as *The Wheel on the School* set in Holland, or *Homecoming*, set in the USA) and folk-tales from another culture (like *Under the Storyteller's Spell*) can illuminate our own. A story about a famous person (like Roald Dahl's autobiographical *Boy*) a novel set in a social context unfamiliar to most readers (such as *The Piemakers*) or even a story about reading, writing and arithmetic (*The Phantom Tollbooth*) can all be very useful in extending children's experience.

Intellectual

In recent years attention has also been focused on the role of stories in cognitive as well as personal and social development, the ways in which we use narrative as a 'supreme means of rendering otherwise chaotic, shapeless events into a coherent whole, saturated with meaning'.[12] We are bombarded with information, ideas, images and sounds through our senses all the time. Normally, much of what we perceive is so familiar that we don't need to think consciously about it, but we have in our minds a framework of understanding of everyday objects and events which we can use to make sense of what we see and experience; or to put it in a rather more formal way: 'Whatever our age, whatever our language, whatever our cultural background, we function psychologically by building systematic representations of experience, which provide both an interpretation (or structuring) of the past and a system for anticipating the future.'[13] Stories play a fundamental part in constructing and maintaining these 'systematic representations', or mental maps:

> Stories contribute to the formation and re-formation in our children of the cultural imagination, a network . . . of patterns and templates through which we articulate our experience. . . . So the stories we tell our children, the narratives we give them to make sense of cultural experience, constitute a kind of mapping, maps of meaning that enable our children to make sense of the world. They contribute to children's sense of identity, an identity that is simultaneously personal and social.[14]

To take a very trivial example, if I look out of my window I can see a quantity of green matter. But I don't just perceive it, I understand what it is and what its implications are, and I can, if necessary, explain my perception to myself or to others with many different but overlapping stories about the nature of what we call grass. For example, one of my stories could be about the reasons why grass is green: probably a rather inadequate narrative of the half-remembered characteristics of chlorophyll. Another might concern my wife's recent assertions of the need to use the mower fairly soon; yet another might be about the different ways I, my children and my dog make use of the grass. In other words, objects and events are obvious and familiar because we can make sense of them by telling stories about them. Similarly, when we are faced with something strange or unfamiliar, the process of making sense, of understanding, usually consists of being able to locate the unknown or the new into our existing mental schemes and structures; we try to construct a story about it which will fit.

An excellent example is provided by 17-year-old Maryla's story about the way in which complex plastics are formed from carbon, of which this is a brief extract:

> One of the curious things about carbon atoms and about most other atoms come to that, is that they appear to behave as though they possess arms, four in the case of carbon, each terminating in an eager hand, ready to grab at some stray hand belonging to another atom, in order to satisfy their perpetual lust for security. Carbon is not only willing to hold hands with members of its own species, i.e. other carbon atoms, but also associates quite readily with members of different species, e.g. hydrogen (which unfortunately for them have only one hand restricting them to monogamy). What is more, if there are relatively few atoms available, one pair can take mutual comfort in holding hands twice, or even three times, to give a double or triple bond respectively. Given the choice, though, the carbon atoms would prefer to hold hands with four different, or separate atoms, rather than waste three hands on the same fella (well, it's only natural, isn't it?).[15]

And so the story goes on, complete with witty cartoon pictures of atoms holding hands. Because I am deplorably ignorant of science this is invaluable, because it transforms what to me are difficult and rather abstract ideas into a coherent and intelligible story which I can make sense of within my existing mental frameworks. (Of course, I know that molecules don't really hold hands, but the story enables me to make sufficient sense for my present purposes.)

Gordon Wells argues on the basis of his major study of young children learning language and literacy that this process of making sense through stories, or 'storying' as he calls it, is a fundamental way in which the human mind works, what Barbara Hardy has called a 'primary act of mind',[16] and thus central to children's learning. Because young children's experience is so limited, because so much of their social and physical world consists of the unfamiliar, the process of building up mental frameworks within which events and ideas and perceptions make sense is absolutely crucial. Wells goes on to illustrate how such storying is essentially social: gradually young children's increasing experience, especially by interacting with others through language, necessitates more subtle and complex stories which in turn are challenged by new information and new ideas.

For example, I was recently asked by a 6-year-old girl how orange juice gets inside oranges. Clearly her experience suggested to her that, on the whole, liquid cannot penetrate solid objects, yet an orange is a solid object without any obvious cracks or holes that is full of liquid. The framework of understanding that the child had built up in her mind from all the stories she knew about liquids failing to pass through solid objects was no longer adequate, because here was an anomaly. As I told her a new and slightly more sophisticated story about the way in which fruit is formed, so the understanding that she had of the nature of the physical world was, to some small extent, increased. Another example comes from a discussion by the four girls quoted earlier of part of Beverly Cleary's *Ramona the Pest*, in which the term 'stroller' is used:

PAULINE: She – wants – a stroller. What's a stroller?

ALICE: A buggy.

GILLIAN: A walking kinda thing, for learning to walk –

PAULINE: A push and ride sort of thing, you mean?

GILLIAN: No, you know –

PAULINE: It's sort of like that.

ALICE: It's a pushchair – it's more or less –

GILLIAN: You know, things like tables with holes in them and you walk around in them.

PAULINE: That's a baby-walker.

ALICE: Jeffrey my wee brother's got one.

And so on, eventually concluding that a stroller must indeed be a baby-walker of some kind.

Wells summarizes the importance of stories for children's learning by arguing that:

> although storying may have its roots in the biologically given human predisposition to construct mental stories in order to make sense of perceptual information, it very quickly becomes the means whereby we enter into a shared world, which is continually broadened and enriched by the exchange of stories with others. In this sense, the reality each one of us inhabits is to a very great extent a distillation of the stories we have shared ... in our perpetual attempts to understand the world in which we live and our experiences in it.[17]

Wells' work clearly has implications for the teacher, and not only for the teacher of literature: if stories are a fundamental way in which we learn it becomes plausible to view other subjects – such as science, history and geography – in part as stories about the physical world, about other times, about other places; and the way in which many of the great religious leaders have incorporated their moral teaching into stories can be seen to make a lot of sense.

Curricular

One of the most important reasons for valuing fiction, particularly for teachers, has not yet been mentioned. This is the crucial relevance of stories to the curriculum and especially to the development of literacy, to children's abilities to read, to write, to talk and to listen.

THE DEVELOPMENT OF READING

First, then, reading stories enables children to develop their reading competence. Reading is not a relatively straightforward skill like swimming or bricklaying but rather a range of complex accomplishments and experiences which extends far beyond the ability to decipher words on a page, important though that is. Even fluent adult readers are still learning to read; none of us ever finish. Here is a simple example which demonstrates how much more there is to reading than decoding print:

> Without derogating from the rights powers or duties of the Trustees as such the Trustees shall during the period of administration be entitled to exercise

as regards any of the property comprised in my estate or over which I shall die possessed of a general power of appointment such powers and discretions as would have been exercisable by my Trustees had the said administration already been completed.[18]

Few adult readers will have much difficulty in reading this in the sense that all the words – with the possible exception of 'derogating', which means detracting – are relatively easy and familiar. But to read it in a way which enables us to make sense of it is quite a different matter. The difficulty we have is partly due to the very complex structure of the sentence and the unusual way in which language is used, and partly because we lack familiarity with the context, with the assumptions the writer makes, and with the knowledge he has of the implications of what he writes. In other words, to understand the passage fully we would have to bring to it both the ability to cope with language used in a complex and sophisticated way and also some specific knowledge of, in this case, the legal requirements relating to the writing of a will.

By the age of 9 or 10 nearly all children have made progress in reading in that they can decode print, admittedly with very varied degrees of skill and fluency. What they lack most of all, and what they and we can spend a lifetime acquiring, is experience both of the almost infinite variety of social life and also the almost infinite variety of ways in which language can be used. Stories, as I have suggested earlier, can make a huge contribution to widening children's experience of life, but they can also enable children to increase their expertise in reading in the fullest sense. Encounters with skilful storytellers provide models of the use of language in a vast range of contexts, a sense of the ways sentences are structured, the proper use of punctuation and its effects, how new and interesting words can be used effectively, how dialogue can be organized, how metaphors and similes are used to heighten an effect, how paragraphs and chapters work, and in general how written language can be formed and shaped for different purposes. Even in the primary school, children can also begin to learn something about the ways in which the author's tone of voice can be detected and his or her point of view identified, the ways in which he or she builds a character and develops a plot, how to detect implications and what the author expects us to understand without direct assertion, and so on.

It may be worth considering an example of the way in which reading fiction can enable children both to become familiar with the way in which stories work and in particular how children can develop the ability to make thoughtful and sensible judgements of the quality of a particular text. This is important not only in the context of children's increasing understanding and appreciation of literature, but also because it increases their ability to discriminate, to be properly critical, which is valuable in many contexts. Two 10-year-old boys are discussing Joan Lingard's *The Twelfth Day of July*:

RONAN: It was easy – I can read other books and they say all these all like posh words – posh words y'know.

MICHAEL: And these words are like the words we use.

RONAN: Slang y'know some of them.

INTERVIEWER: Yes – what kind of books are there that talk posh then?

MICHAEL: Oh y'know the way them *Famous Five* ones they're always so posh y'know.[19]

These boys are showing here the beginnings of an awareness of some of the different ways language can be used in a story, and beginning to assess its appropriateness. In other words, they are developing some of the skills of the thoughtful and critical reader, and starting to engage in the beginnings of literary criticism. In such ways then, by reading and hearing stories children can develop their reading skills and can become better at understanding and responding to all kinds of texts. As Margaret Meek has recently concluded in a cogent and subtle essay, 'the reading of stories makes skilful, powerful readers who come to understand not only the meaning but also the force of texts'.[20]

THE DEVELOPMENT OF WRITING

Not only do readers get better at reading, there are also beneficial effects on other aspects of language development, notably writing. The ways in which children's writing is shaped and formed by what they read is very significant. Children pick up from their reading, in both obvious and quite subtle ways, the conventions and the skills of writing. They can learn how words are spelled, how a sentence is punctuated, how dialogue is written; they extend their working vocabulary by seeing unfamiliar words and phrases used in a meaningful context. In addition, more complex and difficult aspects of writing can begin to be learned: how a story is organized and structured, how a description can be made vivid and alive, how a paragraph can be shaped, and so on. In all such ways, and there are many more, reading provides an inexhaustible resource which can act as an inspiration to write and as a source of ideas and techniques which children can use in their own writing.

THE DEVELOPMENT OF LANGUAGE AND LITERACY

Abilities in reading, writing, speaking and listening do not develop in isolation, because all aspects or modes of language are intimately connected and inextricably interwoven. Much of children's learning about language is through the implicit lessons of what they read; without such working models of language in use children's own language production would be so much the poorer. Thus the more the child reader is exposed to written language in its huge variety of theme, form, style, tone and quality the more his ability to use language also improves: his writing is enriched and the quality of his spoken language is enhanced. As the Kingman Report said, 'such a reception of language allows the individual greater possibilities of production of language',[21] both orally and in writing.

One of the most important reasons for using fiction in schools, then, is because it increases children's abilities to read, write, and use language effectively, and, in the widest sense, contributes to the development of literacy. But finally, before leaving this point, it is worth noting that children who enjoy reading tend to read more; as they read more they get better at reading and writing; and as they get better at it their desire to read and write is reinforced. The whole process can be a virtuous circle in which fiction provides both the initial stimulus and continuing motivation. And this brings us back, once again, to the importance for teachers of recognizing and encouraging children to enjoy and delight in reading and hearing stories, because it is through the pleasures of reading that all the other powerful and important functions of texts begin and can develop.

Conclusion

As our society changes so the place of reading in general and fiction in particular within it changes also. However, for the foreseeable future while written stories continue to have functions and effects which are regarded as valuable it seems certain that they will survive and flourish. There are innumerable reasons why the experience of fiction is valuable, but for present purposes the following seem to be the most important – and it is notable that each to a greater or lesser extent is relevant to children and children's reading as well as to that of adults:

- PERSONAL: reading fiction is enjoyable, and in subtle ways may beneficially affect the character of the reader. In particular, it has been claimed that it can shape the reader's personality, extend or stretch his or her powers of imagination, and develop empathy.
- SOCIAL: our culture is saturated with stories and reading fiction enables the reader to understand more of the nature of society. Fiction enables the reader to explore secondary worlds otherwise impossible of access, and such vicarious experience may inform, reflect or illuminate the reader's own experience.
- INTELLECTUAL: learning through stories (storying) is a fundamental attribute of the human mind and is one of the ways in which unfamiliar or abstract ideas can be made accessible and intelligible in all areas of the school curriculum and beyond.
- CURRICULAR: fiction provides motivation for learning to read and write effectively, and has powerful and positive effects on the reader's literary competences and language development in general.

These reasons why reading fiction is of value have been separated out in this way, although they are all clearly interlinked and mutually reinforcing, in order to provide a context for discussion of the place of fiction in the primary school. Implicit in the argument has been the suggestion that there is much more to using fiction with primary schoolchildren than as a way of providing them with an opportunity to develop or practise their reading skills, although this is one perfectly valid motive. These themes need to be considered in more detail, but first it is necessary to locate the use of fiction in the practice of primary schools, and consider some recent evidence.

References

1 Chandler, D. *Young Learners and the Microcomputer*, Milton Keynes, Open University Press, 1984, p. 27.
2 See for example Trelease, J. *The Read-Aloud Handbook*, Harmondsworth, Penguin, 1984, Ch. 7.
3 Thorpe, D. *Reading For Fun*, Cranfield, Cranfield Press, 1988, p. 147. At the time of writing the best-selling book in the UK is George Eliot's *Middlemarch*, which has just been serialized on television.

4   Landsberg, M. *The World of Children's Books*, London, Simon & Schuster, 1988, p. 17.

5   A good example of this process is provided by Elaine Moss 'The peppermint lesson', in her *Part of the Pattern*, London, Bodley Head, 1986.

6   Department of Education and Science *A Language for Life* (Bullock Report), London, HMSO, 1975, p. 124.

7   This and subsequent quotations from children's discussions are from unpublished work by Harold Brownlow.

8   Fry, D. *Children Talk About Books: Seeing Themselves as Readers*, Milton Keynes, Open University Press, 1985, pp. 94–5.

9   Applebee, A. *The Child's Concept of Story*, Chicago, Chicago University Press, 1978, p. 134.

10 Department of Education and Science/Welsh Office *English for Ages 5 to 16* (2nd Cox Report), London, HMSO, 1989, Ch. 7, para 3. See also Department of Education and Science/Welsh Office *English for Ages 5 to 11* (lst Cox Report), London, HMSO, 1988.

11 Spink, J. *Children as Readers*, London, Clive Bingley, 1989, p. 72.

12 Rosen, B. *And None of It Was Nonsense: The Power of Storytelling in School*, London, Mary Glasgow, 1988, p. 164.

13 Applebee, A. op. cit., 3.

14 Watkins, T. 'Cultural studies, new historicism and children's literature', in Hunt, P. (ed.) *Literature for Children: Contemporary Criticism*, London, Routledge, 1992, p. 183.

15 Burgess, C. *et al.* (eds.) *Understanding Children Writing*, Harmondsworth, Penguin, 1973, pp. 31–2.

16 Hardy, B. 'Towards a poetics of fiction: an approach through narrative', in Meek, M. *et al.* (eds.) *The Cool Web: The Pattern of Children's Reading*, London, Bodley Head, 1977.

17 Wells, G. *The Meaning Makers: Children Learning Language and Using Language to Learn*, London, Hodder & Stoughton, 1987, p. 196.

18 Quoted in McKenzie, M. *Journeys Into Literacy*, Huddersfield, Schofield & Sims, 1986, p. 6.

19 Marriott, S. 'Me Mum she says it's bigotry: children's responses to *The Twelfth Day of July*', in *Children's Literature in Education*, Vol. 16, no. 1, 1985, p. 56.

20 Meek, M. *How Texts Teach What Children Learn*, Stroud, Thimble Press, 1988.

21 Department of Education and Science *Report of the Committee of Enquiry into the Teaching of English Language* (Kingman Report), London, HMSO, 1988, Ch. 2, para 23.

CHILDREN'S BOOKS

ADAMS, RICHARD, *Watership Down*, Puffin.

CARROLL, LEWIS, *Alice's Adventures in Wonderland*, Walker.

CHARLES, FAUSTIN (ed.), *Under the Storyteller's Spell: Folk Tales from the Caribbean*, Puffin.

The Value of Fiction

CLEARY, BEVERLY, *Ramona the Pest*, Puffin.
CLEARY, BEVERLY, *Dear Mr Henshaw*, Puffin.
CONLON-McKENNA, MARITA, *Under the Hawthorn Tree*, Puffin.
CRESSWELL, HELEN, *The Piemakers*, Puffin.
DAHL, ROALD, *Boy*, Puffin.
DE JONG, MEINDERT, *The Wheel on the School*, Puffin.
DESAI, ANITA, *The Village bv the Sea: An Indian Family Story*, Puffin.
GARFIELD, LEON, *Smith*, Puffin.
GODDEN, RUMER, *The Diddakoi*, Piper.
HALLWORTH, GRACE, *A Web of Stories*, Mammoth.
HIGGS, MIKE (ed.), *Dan Dare: Pilot of the Future*, Hawk Books.
JUSTER, NORTON, *The Phantom Tollbooth*, Lions.
LAVELLE, SHEILA, *My Best Fiend*, Young Lions.
LE GUIN, URSULA, *A Wizard of Earthsea*, Puffin.
LEWIS, C.S., *The Lion, the Witch and the Wardrobe*, Lions.
MAGORIAN, MICHELLE, *Goodnight Mr Tom*, Puffin.
NORTON, MARY, *The Borrowers*, Puffin.
SUTCLIFF, ROSEMARY, *The Eagle of the Ninth*, Puffin.
SUTCLIFF, ROSEMARY, *The High Deeds of Finn Mac Cool*, Red Fox.
THOMPSON, BRIAN, *The Story of Prince Rama*, Viking Kestrel.
TOWSEND, SUE, *The Secret Diary of Adrian Mole Aged 13¾*, Methuen.
VOIGHT, CYNTHIA, *Homecoming*, Lions.
WACHTER, ORALEE, *No More Secrets for Me*, Puffin.
WADDELL, MARTIN and DUPASQUIER, PHILIPPE, *Going West*, Andersen.
WHITE, E. B., *Charlotte's Web*, Puffin.

2

Fiction in the Curriculum

Advice and prescriptions for teachers have always been plentiful, but the National Curriculum provides for the first time a legislated framework for classroom work. It is therefore important first to consider in broad outline its suggestions for the use of stories and fiction within the Key Stage 2 curriculum.

Fiction in the National Curriculum

While the use of fiction does feature in subjects such as history and science, in general, and not surprisingly, it is English which is seen by the authors of the National Curriculum as the area of the curriculum in which it plays a central role. Each of the working groups and committees whose reports preceded the publication of the original version of the National Curriculum[1] discussed and advocated the use of literature as an essential feature of the English curriculum, and justified their views with much the same arguments as I have used. The ethos of these reports throughout was one of support for and indeed enthusiastic espousal of the role of literature in the English programme. As a result, fiction was central to the 1990 version of the programmes of study and statements of attainment in English. These documents included abundant reference to and discussion of the use of literature, and not only in material related to reading: the holistic nature of English was much stressed in all the National Curriculum materials. For example, in speaking and listening, many activities relevant to the use of fiction appeared in the statements of attainment, such as: 'listen attentively to stories and poems and talk about them' (level 2), 'relate real or imaginary events in a connected narrative' (level 3), 'expressing a personal view' (level 4), and 'contribute to and respond constructively in discussion' (level 5). Similarly, the writing statements of attainment contained references to children's ability to 'write stories showing an understanding of the rudiments of story structure' (level 2), 'write more complex stories' (level 3), 'write stories which have an opening, a setting, characters, a series of events and a resolution' (level 4), and so on.[2]

Although literature was explicitly considered throughout the English curriculum, it was in the programmes of study and statements of attainment for reading, as one might expect, that it featured most prominently. At Key Stage 2, for example, it was suggested that children should hear stories, select books for reading, read aloud as well as silently, participate in activities related to reading, and begin to respond to what they read and: 'refer to relevant passages to support their opinions'. The programmes of study were accompanied by statements of attainment which in Key Stage 2 were similarly permeated throughout by references to fiction and the use of stories. Pupils should at level 2:

> describe what has happened in a story and predict what may happen next; listen and respond to stories ... expressing opinions informed by what has been read.

At level 3 they should:

> listen attentively to stories, talk about setting, storyline and characters and recall significant detail; demonstrate ... that they are beginning to use inference, deduction and previous reading experiences to find and appreciate meanings beyond the literal; bring to their writing and discussion about stories some understanding of the way stories are structured.

Similarly at level 4 pupils should demonstrate:

> an ability to explore preferences ... that they are developing their abilities to use inference, deduction and previous reading experience.

And at level 5:

> that they are developing their own insights and can sustain them by reference to the text.[3]

The Non-Statutory Guidance for English developed these themes, making many useful suggestions for teachers, such as that children could be helped to respond to their experience of literature by work centred on the plot, the characters, the setting, the theme and the style and genre.[4]

In early 1993 some revisions to the National Curriculum in English were proposed,[5] which provided somewhat different, and rather controversial programmes of study and attainment targets. Further revisions were incorporated into the Consultation Report published later the same year.[6] The most recent official document currently available, published in May 1994,[7] advocates the introduction of yet another version of curriculum requirements to take effect in September 1995, although it remains to be seen whether this takes place as planned. But however the political debate turns out, there is no doubt that children's fiction retains a central place in the new proposals, notably in the provisions for reading.

At Key Stage 2 the new programme of study states:

> Pupils should be encouraged to develop as enthusiastic, independent and reflective readers. They should be introduced to a wide range of literature and non-fiction and be reading extensively for their own interest and pleasure, and for information.
>
> Their reading should include stories, poems, plays, fables, myths and legends, novels. . . . Teachers should develop pupils' reading through the use of progressively more challenging and demanding texts. Opportunities for reading should include both independent and shared reading of play scripts and other texts by groups and the whole class.

The programme of study suggests that pupils' progression can be seen in their 'increasing independence as readers' and 'their understanding and response to what they have read'. Pupils' development of understanding is characterized, it is suggested, by such features as: 'the confidence to choose and read more challenging and demanding texts', an 'increasing sensitivity to meanings beyond the literal', and 'a growing ability to distinguish between more and less significant aspects of a text'. Pupils' developing response to texts is seen in 'their enthusiasm for reading, and ability to express opinions about books', 'their ability to support their view of a story, poem or non-fiction source by reference to a text', 'a growing sensitivity to how a writer uses language to communicate ideas and achieve effects', and 'an awareness of how texts are constructed and themes and images developed'. The programme of study goes on to suggest that literature in this key stage 'should be wide-ranging', and lists of suggested texts are provided, under six headings: modern verse, modern fiction, classic poetry, long-established children's fiction, texts drawn from a variety of cultures and traditions, and myths, legends and traditional stories.[8]

Statements of attainment are now replaced by rather simpler 'level descriptions'. At Key Stage 2 certain 'types and range of performance' are described which pupils should demonstrate in order to indicate achievement at a particular level. At level 2 pupils should be able to 'express opinions about major events or ideas in stories and poems'. At level 3 children should 'show understanding of the main points and explain preferences', and at level 4 they should 'show understanding of significant ideas, themes, events and characters, beginning to use inference and deduction'. And finally, at level 5 pupils should be able to 'show understanding of a range of texts, selecting essential points and using inference and deduction'.

All these official documents which discuss, advocate and prescribe the contents of the English curriculum for primary schoolchildren differ somewhat in their arguments, emphases and detailed provisions. But what they have in common is that they all view the experience of literature – poems, plays, stories – as central to the concerns of English teaching. It is quite clear throughout that for children to encounter literature frequently and regularly, gradually developing their understanding and enjoyment of what they read, is seen as essential, and not some kind of optional extra.

Fiction and the teaching of reading

Much concern about or criticism of the teaching of reading in primary schools has been expressed in the last few years, particularly by politicians and in the media. While much of the comment has been ill-informed and unproductive, the debate has at least focused public attention anew on the importance of the development of literacy in the primary curriculum.

It has, of course, always been the case that primary school teachers have regarded the teaching of reading as one of their central concerns and there is certainly, and not surprisingly, plenty of evidence that primary schools and teachers have always given and continue to give much attention to it. For primary teachers the use of fiction too has always been seen as relevant to the English curriculum, and again especially in the teaching and development of reading. What is relatively new is that the National Curriculum documents provide a legislated framework of expectations for the use of fiction in the context of English in general and reading in particular. It is therefore of particular interest to examine a number of recent publications which provide evidence of the reality of practice in schools and classrooms, and incidentally the extent to which it matches the prescriptions of the National Curriculum.

Most of these reports are centred on concerns about the teaching of reading in general, rather than specifically on the use of children's literature, but they nevertheless make many interesting comments on the ways fiction is used.

Two recently published reports on reading by HM Inspectorate and several other documents by the same authors and their successors from OFSTED, all based on inspectors' substantial programme of visits to schools, are particularly relevant. In both their reports HMI state that primary schools give a high priority to the teaching of reading, and devote considerable time and effort to it. They go on to describe how many primary teachers make effective use of stories, both written and oral, as well as reading scheme material, information books, poetry, and much else in the reading programme, especially for younger children. However, they do also make some critical comments about the use of fiction in reading teaching, echoing similar concerns raised in many earlier studies and reports.[9] For example, the first report when discussing older primary schoolchildren suggests that:

> The majority of children, having achieved at least a satisfactory level of fluency, had left the reading programme to be 'free readers'. Most of their reading experience was from books which they selected from class libraries, read on their own in school and at home, and sometimes evaluated in the form of book reviews and diaries. The teachers monitored the children's reading but too infrequently discussed books with them, and for the majority, reading was individual and inadequate guidance was given on which books to read. . . . There was a widespread assumption that once children had become fluent readers the primary school had done its job and the main task thereafter was to provide opportunities for children to read individually for their own interest enabling the teacher to spend more time with the slower readers.[10]

Apparently, then, the view taken by some teachers is not that one of the significant roles of written stories in the upper primary school is to enable children to become effective readers, but that this is really the only reason for using fiction at all – 'a widespread assumption that once children had become fluent readers the primary school had done its job' – and that therefore once children have learnt to read fairly well there is no need to do much more than to ensure that children 'tick over', reading mainly on their own. There would seem to be two problems here: first, the idea that some children reach a plateau of excellence beyond which no further improvement or development is possible is a very odd one because even the best primary school readers have much more to learn both about literature and about how to read it. Second, if the arguments put forward earlier have any validity, the role of fiction in practising reading is only one of its many functions, and therefore it could and should continue to play a significant role in children's personal, social, cultural, and intellectual development. While the pressures on classroom teachers are intense and ever-increasing, and thus the view of fiction as of essentially utilitarian value is understandable, the criteria teachers use when making decisions about curriculum content clearly have implications for the assessment of children's responses. Limited aims and purposes inevitably produce limited responses from children. While such constraints on the ability of children to gain maximum benefit from the experience of fiction may occur with children of any ability and attainment level, they may be particularly relevant as an example of the way in which the underachievement of the ablest children in primary schools, which has been described in many recent research studies, is perpetuated.[11]

The second HMI report on reading, a year later, echoed many of the earlier comments, but also portrayed classrooms where fiction was more appropriately used and well developed in the context of reading development. They describe classes where:

> teachers placed great value on group discussion using a shared text. The children in these classes were taught to read with expression, to grasp meaning, to offer critical views and consider different interpretations of the text. This sometimes provided an effective way of drawing slower readers into more challenging work and of teaching about structure, style and subtlety in the written word. On other occasions the children talked about books they had read and discussed their own written work or compared versions of the same story as portrayed, for example, in different cultures, in newspapers, or in a book and a film. Sometimes they prepared short talks to be read to and discussed with others.[12]

Similarly, in a recent report by OFSTED Inspectors:

> story sessions, usually held towards the end of the day, frequently involved the whole class in attentive listening to well-read literature. The selection of stories was often very good and drew upon highly acclaimed authors whose writing was enhanced by the excellent quality of book illustration. These sessions often demonstrated the richness of the input as even the youngest pupils became engrossed, concentrating for quite long periods of time on the content

of the story and entering enthusiastically into a dialogue with the teacher and other children about characters and events.[13]

It is noticeable that the teaching and learning activities which HMI commend here, and elsewhere are not at all exotic or bizarre, but perfectly down-to-earth and straightforward. Using fiction for reading development or other purposes, they imply, is little different in principle from any other everyday classroom practice, and often takes the same forms: children collaborating on a task set by the teacher, or discussing what they have read or heard, or comparing and contrasting aspects of their experience, or writing about aspects of their reading. In a study of the use of fiction in several hundred primary schools a few years ago, I found very similar evidence of ways in which fiction is used in the context of reading and other language development activities, and also how it is incorporated into teaching and learning activities in other areas of the curriculum, notably history and topic work.[14]

However, HMI suggest that such valuable attention to literature is not characteristic of all schools, and in particular is not often grounded in a coherent and fully articulated programme within the classroom or the school: 'the prominence given to literature varies widely, particularly in the junior years. Few schools have consistent policies which ensure that children receive a suitably broad and balanced experience of good literature.'[15] And, in another report: 'The development of wide reading in Key Stage 2 was characterized by a lack of those kinds of intervention which might have helped pupils to venture beyond undemanding popular authors, or books associated with favourite television programmes.'[16] In the absence of a policy agreed and implemented by teachers, fiction can easily be neglected in the hectic atmosphere of the average classroom, or, again, children whose reading is relatively skilled and fluent can be assumed to need little in the way of stimulus from the teacher.

Conclusion

For reasons similar to the ones outlined in Chapter 1 the extensive use of fiction is central to the concerns of the National Curriculum in English, and to some extent is put into practice in the day-to-day work of primary schools, especially in the teaching of reading. However, criticisms by HMI and others suggest that children's experience of literature in the primary school, especially as they get older, can be a bit haphazard. Some teachers make deliberate, structured and effective use of fiction in their reading teaching and in other areas of the curriculum to the benefit of their pupils, but in other cases children, particularly the most fluent and skilful readers, may sometimes be left to pursue reading individually and quietly without much input from the teacher. In few schools is children's literary experience planned and co-ordinated from year to year.

These observations suggest that children's experience of fiction needs to be carefully organized, yet the programme has to retain sufficient flexibility to cater for the individual child. There is certainly a need for a strategy at the level of the whole school, or at least at the appropriate key stage, which is developed, articulated and agreed by the staff, and which provides a suitable context for classroom work. There is also clearly a need for more detailed planning for each class of children so that every individual, at whatever level of reading attainment he or she may be, enjoys as rich, stimulating and fulfilling an experience of literature as is possible. This suggests that it would be useful to consider, first, the kinds of school policy which will provide a favourable environment for the use of fiction, and second, what forms of teaching and learning activities are most appropriate for classroom work. These will be the themes of the next two chapters.

References

1 Especially the 'Kingman' Report (Chap. 1, ref. 18) and the two 'Cox' Reports (Ch. 1, ref 8).
2 Department of Education and Science/Welsh Office *English in the National Curriculum (No. 2)*, London, HMSO, 1990, pp. 3–4 and 12–13.
3 *English in the National Curriculum (No. 2)*, pp. 7–9 and 30–1.
4 National Curriculum Council *English Non-Statutory Guidance*, York, NCC, 1990, para D3.
5 Department for Education/Welsh Office *English for Ages 5 to 16 (1993)*, York, NCC, 1993.
6 National Curriculum Council *Consultation Report: English in the National Curriculum*, York, NCC, 1993.
7 Schools Curriculum and Assessment Authority *English in the National Curriculum: Draft Proposals*, London, SCAA, 1994.
8 *Draft Proposals*, pp. 12–14 and 32–3.
9 Most notably in Southgate, V. *et al. Extending Beginning Reading*, London, Heinemann, 1981.
10 HMI *The Teaching and Learning of Reading in Primary Schools*, London, DES, 1991, p. 10.

11 One of the most forceful and persuasive of recent studies of children's classroom experience, based on a large-scale empirical study, is Alexander, R. *Policy and Practice in Primary Education*, London, Routledge, 1992.

12 HMI *The Teaching and Learning of Reading in Primary Schools 1991*, London, DES, 1992, p. 8.

13 OFSTED *English Key Stages 1, 2 and 3: Third Year 1991–2*, London, HMSO, 1993, p. 15.

14 Marriott, S. 'Teachers use of fiction in primary schools in Northern Ireland', *The Irish Journal of Education*, Vol. 20, nos. 1 and 2, 1986.

15 HMI *Aspects of Primary Education: The Teaching and Learning of Language and Literacy*, London, HMSO, 1990, para 21.

16 HMI *English Key Stages 1, 2 and 3: A Report by HM Inspectorate on the Second Year, 1990–91*, London, DES, 1992, p. 13.

3

A Policy for Fiction

As children get older they tend to read fewer stories.[1] This process is most noticeable in the teenage years, but it often begins in the primary school. Of course, the picture is complicated by factors other than age. For example, the evidence suggests that girls tend to read more fiction than boys, and indeed more boys than girls give up voluntary reading altogether. On the whole, boys begin to prefer factual books rather than fiction, or if they do continue to read stories their tastes are sometimes narrowly focused on a few themes and styles: science fiction, for example, or war stories. Generally, however, girls are less interested in information books and more often willing to read a wider range of fiction.[2]

In addition to age and gender other reasons and causes may also be relevant. For example, children may be particularly likely to resist reading if they come from homes where there is little reading by relatives and friends, or if for one reason or another they do not own any books themselves, or belong to a public library.

There are, then, powerful social and cultural influences, particularly from the home, but also from peer groups and from the mass media, which may convince some children, especially boys, that reading stories is of little value. It is clearly difficult, if not impossible, for teachers in primary schools to solve all such problems through even the best school policies. But, as Raleigh[3] has argued, there is also evidence that if children attend a school which doesn't have a decent library, or if it has one it doesn't encourage children to use it, or it has inadequate class library provision, the problems may be exacerbated. Similarly, if children are offered a series of inappropriate books by adults or they see a considerable gap between the kinds of book legitimized in school and the kinds of book they might choose to read themselves if they could find them, the likelihood of the children becoming avid readers is once again diminished. And these certainly are factors within the power of teachers to influence.

Any framework intended to provide an appropriate environment for children's experience of fiction must begin from current circumstances, and therefore a useful starting-point is to examine existing conditions in the school and to consider the extent to which they can or should be changed. It may then be possible to find ways in which matters may be improved or developed. Clearly, since schools and classrooms are so varied not all the following issues will be relevant in every situation, but they are some of the most important factors in providing an appropriate context for successful work with fiction.

Teachers

The most significant resource for teaching using fiction in any school, more important even than books, is the skills, knowledge and experience of the teachers. Any staff, even of very small schools, have between them an enormous amount of experience of fiction, including knowledge of nursery rhymes and versions of fairy stories, folk-tales and fables, a huge fund of anecdotes and stories and verse of all kinds remembered or half-remembered, any number of books read and enjoyed both of children's literature and of fiction for adults; whatever their academic background, all teachers are heirs to the cultural heritage of literature. Just as importantly, of course, almost all teachers have a wealth of experience of children's responses to literature of many kinds, and almost invariably they have a deep understanding of children's abilities and achievements in learning, and a concern that children should learn to read fluently and effectively. These days it is almost fashionable to denigrate teachers' knowledge and experience, but clearly it is the fundamental basis on which classroom work depends in all areas of the curriculum. The knowledge and understanding that teachers already have of children and of stories and of their interaction provides a strong foundation for using fiction in any school, particularly if this accumulated wisdom can be collected together and shared.

If, in addition, at least some of the teachers are convinced of the value of stories within the curriculum, are interested in and enthusiastic about children's literature and regard it as inherently worthwhile, then even more can be achieved. Of course, not every teacher in a primary school can or would wish to devote the time and effort required to gain particular expertise in this area, but even if there is only one such person her enthusiasm can be contagious, and she may be able to provide sufficient knowledge and advice for her colleagues. This in itself can go a long way to improving the ways in which fiction is used.

Libraries

The location and organization of books, and non-book resources, within the school requires some consideration. The crucial factor here is that the policy should ensure maximum availability and accessibility for children. Whether books should be centrally located in a school library, shared in year groups, or divided into classroom collections will obviously depend partly on what physical spaces are most suitable, but each possibility also has advantages and disadvantages in terms of making the most books available to the maximum number of children. A school library enables children to choose from a wider range, and is more cost-effective, but on the other hand it is often by its nature physically removed from the classroom and thus less accessible to each individual, and the sheer quantity of books available can be a bit overwhelming for young and/or inexperienced readers. In contrast, a classroom collection can be more intimate and seem to belong to the children in a more personal way, but on the other hand may not include much range or variety. If it is a practical proposition, a combination of a whole school library and a small class collection of popular books appropriate to the age and interests of the children is often the best compromise.

Whatever decisions are made about the location of books, however, consideration of ways of making books both attractive and accessible to children is important because however beautiful the books are, however expensive they were, and wherever they are situated, they are of no value unless they are read. Even if the school library area is very small, important messages are conveyed to children about the value of books if it is comfortable and inviting – carpets, cushions, soft chairs – and tidy and well organized. The books need to be colourful, in good condition, and arranged attractively on suitable shelving; they should also be changed occasionally, by moving them from classrooms to the central collection and vice versa, so that the collection continues to look fresh and interesting. Mounting simple but stimulating and attractive displays of books in the library or elsewhere in the school is not a difficult proposition. Neatly labelled and imaginatively arranged collections of newly acquired books, or books by the author or illustrator of the week, or 'Year 4's favourite books' perhaps accompanied by some children's work, or stories centred on a particular theme – folk-tales, Christmas books, stories about dinosaurs, and so on – can make a collection seem new and more accessible to children. Needless to say, displays need to change quite frequently, as even the best naturally lose their initial impact after a time.

Children need frequent access to the library for maximum benefit. Providing time for children to browse and to select books, and opportunities to borrow and to read them is probably best organized by having a regular time of the day or week for library based activities for each class, in addition to more casual use, so that this does not get neglected under the pressure of other work. But accessibility means more than just providing time, vital though that is. Adults who use libraries and are familiar with them are often not at all conscious of what forbidding places they can be to the uninitiated. Introducing children to the way in which the library works is thus important in order to demystify the place and the experience, and also because at first sight young children are likely to find library systems totally bewildering. Cataloguing is a prime example: if, for example, a child has enjoyed Mary Hoffman's *Dog Powder* and would like to read another simple animal story, the adult logic of shelving by author's surname is not immediately helpful. Children need therefore to be gradually introduced into the ways that books are organized and to the system that the library uses, preferably through a regular and methodical programme. As the latest version of the National Curriculum specifies, 'Pupils should be taught to use library classification systems, catalogues and indexes'.[4]

Consideration may also need to be given to making provision for children's particular needs by, for example, having a simple subject index on popular themes, or by organizing sub-collections of books, such as picture books or myths and legends or animal stories, on a separate shelf. Brief lists of selections of good books arranged by genre or reading level can also be very helpful. Arrangements may also need to be made to ensure that advice from an adult – a parent? – is available as often as possible to help younger children find their way around the library. In such ways children can gradually become more confident in their ability to use the library and thus they are likely to be more willing to explore and use it.

As children become more used to the library and the way it works they can also valuably participate in all the activities mentioned so far: not only can their efforts be helpful to less experienced children, but they themselves are enabled to learn yet more about library and information handling skills. There often seems to be a direct and positive relationship between the involvement of children in library activities and their enthusiasm for reading.

For all these reasons arrangements need to be made within the school for simple and efficient routines for library use. For a whole school collection this may involve one teacher in planning and organizing a system in collaboration with other members of staff, perhaps with the help of parents or older pupils. Such questions as the location of the library, its furnishings, how books are to be stored, catalogued and arranged, how they are to be issued and deployed, how the library is to be staffed, how children can be introduced to the ways in which books are organized, and how the library can be promoted and made most appealing to children need to be discussed and appropriate action taken. All this takes time and energy, but if we believe, as I have suggested, that reading fiction is central to the concerns of the primary school, it is well worth the effort.[5]

A wide variety of arrangements for collections of books of any kind is possible, and which is most appropriate will largely depend on local circumstances but, to repeat the point, whatever books there are available should be made attractive and accessible to children, since they are only of any use at the point when children are enabled to use them. This is particularly important for the many children who, for one reason or another, do not come from book-filled homes and never use a public library; such children may depend almost entirely on the school's resources for access to books of any kind.

Criteria for choosing books

Just as it is worthwhile to involve children in library activities, so it is useful to enable them to participate in decisions about what fiction books to buy for the school and classroom collections. Not only does this enable children to express real choices and thus become personally involved and committed to the books, but it can also provide some meaningful lessons: looking at what is and is not available already in the library, setting priorities for new acquisitions, finding out and understanding something of the way catalogues, publishers and bookshops work, discussing possibilities and justifying a point of view with other children, negotiating a consensus, and even perhaps learning about the processes of budgeting and ordering.

In most cases, however, it is teachers who are likely to have the most significant role in deciding what should be purchased or otherwise acquired for use in school. While in general it's best to be eclectic and to give almost any book the benefit of the doubt if there is a possibility that it may encourage children to develop the reading habit, nevertheless quite often in practice teachers do need to make judgements and choices. For example, when stocking or restocking a school or a classroom collection choices have to be made from the huge range of children's books in print at any one time. Similarly, an individual teacher usually has a very limited budget, and she will therefore want to spend money on reading materials for classroom use that are fairly sure to be popular with children. Or the teacher may need a set of books for discussion with the whole class or with a group, or a child may ask for advice on a suitable book to read next. On some occasions the teacher may want to find books which will extend children's range and variety of reading, or a story which could usefully introduce a child to new and more challenging material. In such circumstances, unfortunately, there is no infallible substitute for reading a wide range of children's books and combining such experience with knowledge of children's enthusiasms and competences. As Meek says: 'There is, I fear, no short cut for any of us, teachers and parents alike. We have to know the books and the child to match them in terms of the complicated individuality of both'.[6] Nevertheless, for those many occasions when teachers have to make decisions in less than ideal circumstances some criteria, even if neither definitive nor exhaustive, may be helpful in making an informed choice.

PHYSICAL CHARACTERISTICS

Children, and many adults, tend to gain an initial impression of a book when browsing by a quite cursory examination of the front cover picture and title, and perhaps the blurb, contents page or chapter headings. This impression usually determines very quickly whether or not the book is regarded as worth reading. The physical appearance and condition of the book is therefore important, and old, tatty and battered copies of books are inherently unattractive. The front cover illustration tends to have a great impact on children's assessment of a book, often more than that of the title or author, and it therefore needs to be colourful, interesting and appealing, but not very obviously gender-specific: a cover picture of boys playing football may immediately deter girls even if the book is actually of interest to both sexes – for example, the recent Puffin edition of Bernard Ashley's *All My Men*. In relation to illustrations in general, I have discussed at length elsewhere[7] their importance in children's books, not only in books for beginning readers, and need only repeat here that the interaction of quality pictures with a good story adds immeasurably to the impact and effect.

Short books, or collections of short stories, are often more likely to be attractive to young readers than long novels, because the development of reading stamina takes a long time. For many children the experience of actually finishing a story, however brief, is in itself a cause for satisfaction, and in some cases a reason for public rejoicing! Whatever the length of the story, if the pages consist of small dense print without breaks or illustrations this in itself may be enough to discourage a child. The book should also be clearly and legibly printed – appropriate size and style of typeface, colour of print and background, etc. – on good quality paper, should be strongly bound to survive the rigours of classroom use, and in general should give good value for money whether in paper or hardback. It's perhaps surprising how many books fail such simple tests, particularly from certain paperback publishers.

LANGUAGE AND READABILITY

The language and readability of texts for children is clearly crucial to children's experience of reading stories, but it is very difficult to assess in a way which takes account of all the relevant factors. A number of attempts have been made to devise a simple test (or 'readability formula') which can be applied by teachers to assess the language of texts. These usually work by counting the length of words and/or of sentences in a passage and assuming that the longer each is the harder it is to read. But this is at best a very unreliable guide, since generally it is not the length of words, nor even their unfamiliarity, which causes the most difficulty, but rather the structure and syntax of the text, and the concepts which are stated or implied within the story. For example, 'Had he but known, all was not lost' is a short sentence composed of short words, but it is of such complexity that many children would find it hard to understand. On the other hand, a very long sentence whose clauses are connected with 'ands' or 'buts' might be relatively easy to read – 'The boy got up and ran along the path and saw a dog and . . .'

Margaret Donaldson has provided several examples of ways in which the syntax and structure of a text can cause difficulties. She quotes evidence that when 7-year-olds were asked to read 'The girl standing beside the lady had a blue dress', most of them claimed that it was the lady who was dressed in blue, whereas when the sentence read: 'The girl had a blue dress and she was standing beside the lady', nearly all of them got it right. Similarly, in a more recent study, Donaldson cites several sentences which are, she says, typical of written rather than spoken language, and which are very difficult for children to understand; for example:

'The prince, for that is who he was, took her hand.

Sue was not a girl to give up readily.

The ogre's eyes fell upon the floor.

Darkness was upon the face of the deep.'

Donaldson concludes that 'there exists, in effect, a rich and complex "language of books" ',[8] which children need to be exposed to very gradually.

One further consideration, of course, is that even language which is easy to read in the sense that children can accurately and fluently decode the print and make sense of the structure of the text can refer to concepts beyond their understanding: most could probably read 'the speed of light', but neither they, nor many adults, are likely to have any real conception of what it means.

Clearly it is important to provide children with reading material whose language, structure and implied concepts are accessible, but on the other hand the logical outcome of determined attempts to simplify texts can be the insipid banality of the language in some abridgements of the classics of children's fiction, or the extraordinarily stilted and contrived language typical of old-fashioned reading schemes. Such texts are certainly readable, but they are not worth reading because the language is so boring and often much of the sense of story is lost.

Perhaps the most important consideration is to ensure that the language of the text is, initially at least, as close as possible to the rhythms and structures of children's natural use of language in speech, because the written word used in ways similar to spoken language is much easier for children to read and understand. For this reason much of the story in well-written and popular books for children is often carried in lively dialogue rather than in lengthy passages of description or reflection. If, in addition, the language of the story flows in a way which draws the reader into the story, if it is linguistically alive, if it reads aloud well, then it is more likely to be easily accessible. Most authors of children's books write in a style which is more direct and simple than is typical of fiction for adults, but the best ones also use language just as flexibly and vividly.

Many further criteria have been suggested,[9] but in practice it is usually quite easy to assess without readability tests whether children find the language of a book bewilderingly difficult, or readable, attractive and engaging; what is certain is that if the story is powerful and exciting, children can often cope with more complex and difficult grammar, syntax and vocabulary than could otherwise be expected.

STORY

For most readers of fiction it is the story which makes the book worth reading, and so a strong and convincing plot is needed, with clear lines of development and which relate to experience that children can recognize. The story should have plenty of action, a clear and definite point, suspense, credible relationships and believable characters. Children, and probably adults too, enjoy reading about characters that they can identify with, especially ones who behave as they might like to rather than as they actually do; think of the appeal of *Dennis the Menace*, or Angela, the naughty girl in *My Best Fiend*, or the James Bond books for that matter.

If fiction has an important role in personal and social development, then the story should have some relevance to children's inner world of imagination and make-believe, as well as to everyday life. This implies that they should have the opportunity to read, for example, ancient and modern myths and legends, fantasy and fairy tales, as well as stories set in the gritty reality of the here and now.

Humour is an important ingredient of the enjoyment of stories for children – even if their humour is often of a rather basic and earthy kind! – and so sometimes is sadness and pathos. But whatever emotion is stirred, if the story is direct and exciting and relevant to children's interests, it is more likely to be attractive, and therefore more likely to be read. If possible, too, as the second Cox Report suggests: 'the story should be capable of interpretation at a number of different levels, so that children can return to the book time and time again with renewed enjoyment in finding something new.' But also as the report goes on immediately to say: 'Most important, the books selected must be those which children enjoy.'[10]

SOCIAL AND MORAL ISSUES

Books need to deal with social and moral issues sensitively and positively. The ways in which gender roles, family relationships, ethnic groups, social

43

class, old age, disability, environmental issues, religious and ethical questions and so on are treated in children's books is often rather controversial.[11] It is still the case that the central assumptions of many children's books tend to be essentially White, male and middle class. Many children's books omit real and meaningful characters from non-White ethnic groups altogether, or feature them as marginal to the story, or present them only in terms of their difference, as problematic or even as exotic. Many other books are set in middle-class social contexts of relative privilege, which is subtly assumed to be the norm, and in which characters whose culture and lifestyle is different are again either absent or even disparaged. Others feature boys always taking active or leadership roles in contrast to passive and subordinate females, or assumptions are made about a limited range of appropriate roles and behaviour for either girls or boys or both. To take just one example, it's amazing how many children in fiction have a Dad who goes out to work and a Mum who stays at home doing housework. Yet this is the reality of family life for only a minority of present-day primary children: think of divorced parents, unemployed fathers, working mothers, one-parent families, adopted children . . .

There are sometimes problems of overtly racist or sexist attitudes in well-known stories written many years ago, when social attitudes were very different from today, by well-known authors like Hugh Lofting, Enid Blyton, W. E. Johns, and others. Such blatant prejudices are much rarer in modern children's books, but it is possible to find plenty of recently published stories in which the explicit or implicit portrayal of the social world fails to reflect the fact that Britain is a multi-ethnic, socially heterogeneous and culturally plural society in an accurate and balanced way. There are rather few children's books, for example, which use as social context the ordinary lives and families of Indian or Chinese children living in Britain, or provide positive images of the experience of growing up in a one-parent family, or in which a leading boy character is portrayed as gentle, quiet and sensitive, or in which the economic and social relationships of different communities provides a theme.

These issues are important because, as I suggested earlier, one of the ways in which children define themselves and their place in society is through the experience of stories, which, if they are misleading or unbalanced, can lead many children to feel excluded or constrained or even inferior – and, conversely, others to feel superior. Thus, at the very least, the reading matter we present to children should include characters and situations with which children from different social groups can identify. For this reason, more stories are needed which feature characters from many ethnic and cultural backgrounds placed in a wider range of social and physical contexts, which present positive images of human diversity, and which do not set stereotyped limits to behaviour, particularly of boys or girls.

The availability and use of fiction, based on a variety of cultural assumptions, is also important for another reason: such stories enable all readers, from whatever social or ethnic background, to broaden their horizons and extend their experience. Since young children's knowledge and experience is inevitably very limited, stories can provide an appropriate sense of the ways in which individuals, families and communities are to some extent dissimilar, and in other, perhaps more fundamental, respects very much alike. The use of folk-tales, myths and legends from a variety of countries and cultures can be very useful for this purpose, as they often provide another way of looking at everyday life, or an unfamiliar perspective on common human concerns.

Children's books also have some part to play in establishing a framework of moral principles for children, because as Harold Rosen has asserted, all stories 'carry in their sub-texts affirmations of what it means to be a proper person and what constitutes proper behaviour',[12] and the ethical messages implied by stories are thus significant. This is not often a major problem in books that primary schoolchildren are likely to read (although there are some novels for teenage readers whose moral implications seem very dubious) but on occasion there may be valid reasons for a teacher to decide that a book is undesirable on these grounds, although censorship would perhaps only be defensible in extreme and rather rare cases.

Summary

A quick assessment of any children's book needs to take into account at least five issues:

- Is the book physically attractive? Are the illustrations of good quality?
- Is the book well written? Is the language vivid and original yet accessible and easy to read?
- Does the book have a powerful story? Is it coherent, convincing and enjoyable?
- Are the book's social and moral assumptions, both explicit and implicit, positive and constructive?

- Is it a book that children will like?

There are plenty of books which fulfil these criteria, many of which are listed in Appendix 1 (pp. 130–8), and some are also discussed in more detail in Chapter 6.

In addition to the intrinsic qualities of any particular book, decisions are often necessary in terms of the contribution each makes to the school or classroom collection as a whole. Essentially this means considering whether a book contributes to the breadth and balance of the collection, and its range and variety.

Range and variety

Observation of children's preferences and discussion with them about the books that they have read and enjoyed can inform choices of books for the school and the classroom. Almost certainly a great range and variety of books will be immediately popular and therefore need to be incorporated into the classroom or school libraries. But even if the collections are biased towards the known interests and enthusiasms of a particular group of children, they also need to be as varied as possible. For one thing, the provisions of the latest proposals for the National Curriculum require the availability of a wide range of types of fiction. But, in addition, it is also important to plan for the fact that children can only read and enjoy what is available, and thus if certain types of story are omitted, children's reading and possible enjoyment is necessarily restricted. It is surprisingly easy to do this, often without realizing it; all teacher readers have likes and dislikes, and the temptation when buying or acquiring books is to choose certain genres and styles and neglect others. For example, I am not very keen on science fiction and would not naturally buy such books myself, but many children find such stories irresistible. And at one time I worked in a school whose school library had an extraordinary number of titles about yachts and sailing – guess what the headteacher's consuming passion was! This is a good reason for making sure that the decisions about what books are to be made available are shared among several teachers, and if possible children too: there is then at least a better chance of a wide range of material being selected.

Some of the categories which will need to be included have already been mentioned, but it will probably also be necessary to include examples of books which fulfil some further criteria.

GENRE AND TYPE

There should be some examples of stories within each of the well-known genres of children's literature: history, adventure and mystery, ghosts and the supernatural, fantasy and science fiction, stories about school, family life and relationships, stories about animals, and so on. In addition to these and other familiar themes, there should be some stories which take conflicts or issues or problems as at least one of their topics; e.g. environmental issues, family relationships; as well as, for reasons suggested earlier, a wide selection of folk-tales, fairy stories, fables, myths and legends.

A range of different forms or types of fiction will be needed: for example, books of short stories and novels of varied length, books of prose extracts, anthologies of verse and books in play format, picture-books and books with fewer or no illustrations, and comic and cartoon books – sometimes referred to as 'graphic novels'. A mixture of very short books, some of medium length and others rather longer, will almost certainly be necessary.

CONTEXT AND CHARACTERS

Stories need to be located within families or lifestyles of different types, and in urban, suburban and rural contexts. Some stories should be set in different historical periods, in other countries or cultures, or within unfamiliar parts of our own society. In addition, there should be some stories set in imaginary or possible worlds, or in the real world as it might be in the future.

Stories about ordinary as well as unusual children are valuable, as are books that have characters with whom children from a variety of different social and ethnic groups can identify. Some of the stories should have interesting and attractive girl as well as boy characters; and stories should not incorporate stereotyped portrayals of male or female behaviour. Some stories should have good and bad characters who are rather more subtle than those where villains and heroes are sharply drawn.

STYLE AND LANGUAGE

Many of the books are likely to be funny or sad, exciting, stimulating or even a little scary. Others may be thought-provoking rather than stirring the emotions; at least some should centre on feelings or on relationships, as well as those mostly concerned with action and plot.

All stories need to use language in an interesting and appropriate way: many will be written in a direct and straightforward style, but some should be rather more complex and elaborate. Some stories should have language which is powerful and energetic, while others may be written in a rather more sophisticated and even ambiguous manner. In the same way, some stories need to be simple and easily accessible, while others should extend children's vocabulary and stretch their powers of comprehension. The recent revised proposals for the National Curriculum make a similar point by suggesting that children should increasingly encounter books 'with challenging subject-matter which broadens perspectives and extends thinking', stories 'with more complex narrative structures and sustained ideas', and texts which incorporate 'figurative language'.[13]

INTEREST LEVEL

It will be necessary to provide some stories that are likely to be attractive to children whose reading competence is very limited, and there will be a need for books which will appeal to really good readers, and titles appropriate for children at all the stages and gradations in between these extremes will also be required. Some stories that will be of particular interest to older or younger children, to girls and/or boys, some that are easy to read and some that are more challenging, at every level of reading ability, are also likely to be useful.

SUMMARY

In addition to the criteria suggested earlier for the assessment of individual books, any collection for use by children in the upper primary school should ideally incorporate variety in at least the following ways:

- GENRE: providing a range of topics and subject matter;
- TYPE: providing different story forms;
- CONTEXT: enabling vicarious experience of a variety of cultures and situations;
- CHARACTERS: about interesting, attractive or intriguing people;
- STYLE: provoking an emotional or intellectual response;
- LANGUAGE: using language in a fresh and original way;

- INTEREST LEVEL: fulfilling the needs of children of diverse attainments.

Examples of books which fulfil these criteria are discussed in Chapter 6, and more are listed in Appendix 1 (pp. 130–8).

ENSURING RANGE AND VARIETY

Clearly a full analysis in these terms of the books in even a relatively small school collection would be a huge job. But in practice the task is much more straightforward, since even on a superficial examination it will usually be clear that there are both gaps and strengths, and once again this is a task to which children can contribute. It will probably be fairly obvious, for example, if many of the books are old and tired, or if there is a lack of suitable material for children whose reading ability is very limited, or if there are no picture-books for older readers. If, in addition, over a period of time the collection is examined more closely in terms of one or two dimensions or themes, such as the quality of the books of myths and legends, or the proportion that have strong female characters, or the extent to which very simple stories are nevertheless well written, the task becomes a little more manageable, if not exactly easy.

Providing reading resources

Providing more and better books for children's use is of obvious importance. A hundred titles for each class of children has been suggested as a minimum,[14] and there will need to be more than one copy of some titles if a book is particularly popular, or if it is to be used as the focus of a class or group activity. Even if looked after carefully, and even if their working life is extended by the use of plastic covers, books that children like and which are therefore much used do have a finite life-span – although in some schools old copies of good books are broken up into separate pages and used as resource material for varied purposes. In addition, of course, the kind of qualitative reviews of stock I have suggested are likely to result in some books being discarded. Like many teacher readers, I find it almost physically painful actually to throw books away however bedraggled or unsuitable they may be, but it is always possible to send them to a jumble sale, or to hold a small second-hand book sale for school funds, unless the books are being thrown out because they are socially or morally unacceptable. Thus there are three kinds of problem: replacing good and popular books that are just worn out, replacing material that is of poor quality even if it is in good physical condition, with better and different books, and adding to the school's resources with new and worthwhile publications.

New books, especially in hardback, are expensive and finances are always tight in primary schools, given the competing demands on limited funds. Such pressures are unlikely to ease in an era of local financial management, and money for story-books is especially vulnerable at times of radical curriculum change when new and expensive priorities emerge in schools, like information technology in recent years. In the end, the quantity of books bought from the school's resources and the extent to which money raised by parental contributions of various kinds can be dedicated to buying more copies will depend on the priority that teachers give to such purchases. Generally, evidence from HMI suggests that teachers do give a high priority to the acquisition of books, but that in some cases rather too little is spent on fiction for older readers in Key Stage 2.[15]

It is unlikely to be possible to do everything at once, and a plan for the gradual improvement of the book collection will be needed, whereby this year funds are focused on increasing the range and variety of, for example, story-books for younger, less fluent readers, whereas next year money will be spent on books with multi-ethnic relevance, and so on.

In general, hardbacks are better than paperbacks, partly because they last longer, and partly because the quality of production of paperbacks is sometimes poor, most noticeably in picture-books. But, on the other hand, it's possible to get two or three paperbacks for the cost of one hardback, and this may often be an overriding consideration. Probably a mixture is best, such as hardbacks for perennial favourites and for picture-books, paperbacks otherwise, although in practice it is often difficult to stick to a hard and fast rule.

As well as using school funds, there are several other ways of acquiring books for classroom use. Good quality copies can often be found in second-hand bookshops, parents and children may be willing to donate unwanted or grown out of books to the school, and more worthwhile than any other source, the local library service can be asked to provide fiction as well as information books for topics and projects, if they do not already do so. Books from the schools' library service are particularly useful: they can provide variety and a sense that the collection is not static and unchanging; they can be used to fill gaps that money can't yet be found for, or for temporary needs such as a class project; and they provide an opportunity to assess the usefulness (or lack of it) of new books, which can inform future purchases.

Keeping abreast of children's books is a massive, if not impossible, task for one person, since hundreds of new books are published each year to add to the thousands already in print. But there are ways of easing the burden: finding at least one interested colleague to share the work is probably the most helpful. Reviews of books in the national press and in specialist magazines like *Books for Keeps* are sometimes helpful. Browsing in book exhibitions, bookshops and libraries provides a sense of what is new, what is available and what is of value. Informal discussions can be held with colleagues, pupils, parents and most of all with public librarians, whose professional expertise is invaluable yet often neglected by teachers. Their advice is often particularly illuminating because other sources of information, notably publishers' catalogues for obvious reasons, tend to promote new books regardless of their quality, rather than others which may have been available for a long time and proved their worth.

Some schools have also built up useful collections of non-book materials for children to read, such as comics, magazines and appropriately printed and bound collections of children's own writings.[16] These are often regarded by children whose reading is not strong as more accessible than even the least forbidding published book, and are thus particularly useful for such children. Audio-visual versions of stories, such as videotapes, audiotapes and computer-based versions of stories are also often very valuable for classroom use. Audiotapes in particular, in which a professional actor reads a story, are cheap, plentiful, and usually of good quality. Many more schools could valuably begin to accumulate such collections, although they do require organization, and thus time, in addition to normal library management.

Promoting books

Attractive and accessible books are vital, but means have also to be found of constantly promoting and publicizing them in ways analogous to those used in advertising; in a sense, 'selling' the pleasures of reading to children. While teachers and books are the most significant aspects of a school literature policy, two other issues are worth considering at this stage as ways in which fiction can be promoted both at home and at school.

SCHOOL ACTIVITIES

Whole school activities which draw attention to books or feature them in some way are very useful, and there are a large number of possibilities. There is a strong association between owning books and enthusiasm for reading, perhaps partly because spending real money on a book is a powerful motivation to read it; and thus developing ownership of books is one important aspect of creating committed readers. Many children come from homes where book buying and using libraries are rare or unknown events, and relatively few children live in an area where there is a good children's bookshop at all. For this reason school schemes which encourage book buying are very worthwhile. Perhaps the most common is the use of one of the book clubs organized by a number of commercial firms so that children can regularly buy a story-book. Such clubs are relatively easy for a busy teacher to organize, although they do have some disadvantages: the range of books offered to children is sometimes rather narrow, and the children do not have the chance to see the books before ordering and so can sometimes be disappointed by what they receive. Other projects, like setting up a school bookstall or bookshop, organizing book fairs, book weeks and so on, are all very beneficial and need not involve an enormous amount of work if they are organized on a fairly small scale at first, especially if the work can be shared among more than one teacher. For example, it may be possible to arrange with a local bookseller to display some of his books on a parents' evening, or for an afternoon in the school hall for children to browse and buy. It's sensible to get detailed advice and help with such projects, which is readily available. Some suggestions of sources of information can be found in Appendix 2 (pp. 139–40).

Visits by authors of children's books to read and talk about their work are also organized by some schools. These are particularly valuable, since they bring home to children in a very direct way the fact that books do not appear from thin air but are actually written by real people, and that published writers have just the same kinds of struggles with their writing as do children themselves. It's also just very interesting for children – and adults – to meet and talk with people who are by definition expert creators of stories. On the whole, writers of children's books welcome contact with schools, as long as they are not overwhelmed by requests for visits, since it keeps them in touch with their audience. Of course, if one is inviting an author it has to be planned carefully so that maximum benefit is achieved, and thought given to all the detailed arrangements that may need to be made.[17] The general consensus among teachers seems to be that such visits are exhausting for everyone concerned, but when they go well they have immense and long-term benefits in terms of the effect on children's reading. Of course, such personal contact with authors is not always possible, for all sorts of reasons: if this is the case, one alternative is to use audiovisual resources (notably the Authorbank videos published by the Book Trust: see Appendix 2) which are very well done, though obviously not as good as personal contact.

One of the most worthwhile activities, and one of the least onerous for the teacher, is to develop relationships with the local public library. In my experience, a librarian who is interested in children's books is worth her weight in gold. Regular class visits are very useful, especially if, as is usually the case, the librarian is able and willing to arrange a programme of activities for the children. Such visits enable children to come into contact with a much wider selection of books than is available in school, to learn something of the way libraries are organized, perhaps to see new and attractive books that are not yet available in school, to hear a story from a new collection, and so on. Librarians can, of course, also encourage children to join, which is particularly valuable for those children from families who do not normally use the library.

PARENTS

The importance of parental involvement in literacy development is increasingly acknowledged, especially for very young children. Yet in the experience of many teachers parental interest in reading, even if almost obsessive in the early years, tends to diminish, often to vanishing-point, as children's reading develops. And so partnership activities between home and school which valuably consolidate and supplement the work of the Key Stage 1 teacher often tend to fade away in the middle and upper primary school, which is a great pity since sustaining the reading habit is so important. Common sense suggests that an active interest by parents in the development of older children's reading is very important; children continue to need support and encouragement from home as well as school. Much research evidence confirms this: for example, a recent study of junior schools found that the effect of parents reading to their children, hearing them read, and providing them with books to read at home was powerful and positive.[18] Similarly, the beneficial impact of such parental support is 'huge' according to HMI in their recent reports on reading.[19]

There are many ways of developing productive relationships with parents, but in most cases the first is likely to be by providing intelligible information and helpful suggestions of various kinds. It is still surprisingly frequent to find that parents have little or no real idea of what goes on in classrooms of older children. So, first and foremost, parents need to be informed clearly about the ways in which the teaching and learning of literacy is organized and structured, most conveniently by the provision of leaflets or booklets explaining the work of the school; this information can be supplemented by personal contact whenever possible. Further, parents often need to be encouraged to act as appropriate role models for their children's reading. The fact that parents are seen reading, enjoying reading, and making use of reading in everyday family contexts is a powerful motivation for children. Advice about appropriate books and authors to look out for in the public library and suggestions of suitable books to buy for children or to give them for birthday or Christmas presents are also helpful; some parents simply do not know what books their children are likely to read and enjoy. Similarly, parents can be alerted to the connections between televised stories or film versions and the books on which they are based, and so on.

The stage beyond providing such information to parents is that of encouraging their interaction with their child's learning through forms of collaboration with the school. Perhaps the most obvious and easily organized form of interaction is by children taking their current school reading-book home to continue with; some schools also have a special collection of books for leisure reading which children can borrow for use at home, which is particularly valuable for children who do not belong to a public library. Parents can usefully be encouraged at least to provide space and time for their child's reading at home, and if possible to take a more active role by talking to the child about his or her reading, by child and parent sharing the reading of a story they can both enjoy, or simply by parents continuing to regularly read stories aloud. (Many parents seem to stop reading stories to their children around the age of 6 or 7, which is a great pity; I suspect that if they continued as long as their children wanted them to, the age would be around 11 or even older.) Similarly, children could be encouraged to bring books from home to read in school or to share with other children, although the teacher may need to quietly control this to prevent the very offensive material that 11-year-olds sometimes acquire circulating in the classroom. Slightly more

ambitious schemes like maintaining a written dialogue between home and school about children's progress in reading, asking parents to finance a book a month from the book club for their child, and so on, are also very useful.

The third stage, in those many schools where parents have become closely and routinely involved in school and classroom work, may entail parents listening to readers and working with individuals or groups in the classroom, or the rather less common idea of parents reading to groups of children. It could involve teachers arranging specific reading-related events for parents: assemblies, book displays, parents' evenings, demonstrations of approaches to reading, etc. In some schools this is taken even further by asking parents to participate in class visits to the local public library, or to help in the organization and management of the school library, or even to take responsibility for running a school bookshop or book-related school events of various kinds.[20] In addition, it should not be overlooked that parents' groups can be encouraged to raise money through fund-raising projects; at least some of the proceeds of such activities could be used for the purchase of new and better books for school or class collections.

In all such ways the messages coming from home can reinforce those from school: that books, stories and reading are central to the purposes of learning. Reading is for life, not just for school!

Conclusion

School policies of any kind are only really effective when they are clear and simple, based on existing practice and realistic about the possible scope and pace of change. And, most important of all, they only really work well when they are based on the outcome of discussions to which all members of staff contribute and which therefore form a set of collective judgements and decisions to which everyone is committed. The construction and application of such a policy is not easy but is very worthwhile as it provides a useful framework within which the classroom work of individual teachers can take place. I have suggested that such a policy needs to consider:

- What knowledge of and interest in children's books exists among staff and how it can be shared and increased.
- How existing resources can best be located, arranged and organized in order to promote the maximum accessibility and availability of books.

- How the stock of books can be added to and improved, and how appropriate criteria can be used in order to select more and better books for children of differing abilities, attainments and interests.
- What whole school activities for promoting fiction reading are feasible and worth while.
- How parents can be productively involved in the development of fiction reading.

Many of these issues have obvious implications for the work of individual teachers and their pupils in the classroom. In Chapter 4 classroom practice will be considered in more detail.

References

1 The APU survey *Attitudes to Reading at Age 15* (London, DES, 1987) states that: 'for about a quarter of the pupils in their last year at school, reading is decidedly not a regular source of pleasure'.
2 See Gorman, T. *Pupils' Attitudes to Reading*, London, NFER/Nelson, 1987.
3 Raleigh, M. 'Independent reading', in *The English Magazine*, No. 10, Autumn 1982, p. 22.
4 Schools Curriculum and Assessment Authority *English in the National Curriculum: Draft Proposals*, London, SCAA, 1994, p. 13.
5 An excellent resource for teachers considering better use of libraries is Gawith, G. *Library Alive!*, London, A. & C. Black, 1987.
6 Meek, M. *Learning to Read*, London, Bodley Head, 1982, pp. 133–4.
7 Marriott, S. *Picture Books in the Primary Classroom*, London, Paul Chapman, 1991.
8 Donaldson, M. 'Literature and language developments, in Hoffman, M. *et al.* (eds.) *Children, Language and Literature*, Milton Keynes, Open University Press, 1982, p. 18, and 'Sense and sensibility: some thoughts on the teaching of literacy', in Beard, R. (ed.) *Teaching Literacy, Balancing Perspectives*, Sevenoaks, Hodder & Stoughton, 1993, p. 45.
9 For example, a summary is provided by Beard, R. *Developing Reading 3–13* (2nd edn), London, Hodder & Stoughton, 1990, p. 124.
10 Department of Education and Science/Welsh Office *English for Ages 5 to 16* (2nd Cox Report), London, HMSO, 1989, para 7.12.
11 See, for example, Klein, G. *Reading into Racism*, London, Routledge & Kegan Paul, 1985; Leeson, R. *Reading and Righting*, London, Collins, 1985; Dixon, B. *Catching Them Young* (Vols. 1 and 2) London, Pluto, 1977.
12 Quoted in Meek, M. and Mills, C. *Language and Literacy in the Primary School*, London, Falmer Press, 1988, p. 148.
13 Schools Curriculum and Assessment Authority *English in the National Curriculum: Draft Proposals*, London, SCAA, 1994, p. 13.

14 Somerfield, M., Torbe, M. and Ward, C. *A Framework for Reading: Creating a Policy in the Primary School*, London, Heinemann, 1983, p. 34.

15 HMI *The Teaching and Learning of Reading in Primary Schools 1991*, London, DES, 1992, p. 13; HMI *English Key Stages 1, 2 and 3: A Report by HM Inspectorate on the Second Year, 1990–91*, London, DES, 1992, p. 28; OFSTED *English Key Stages 1, 2 and 3: Third Year 1991–2*, London, HMSO, 1993, p. 23.

16 See for example, Children of Earls Barton Junior School *All Four One*, Northampton, Earls Barton Junior School, 1986.

17 Helpful details are provided in Chambers, A. *The Reading Environment*, Stroud, Thimble Press, 1991.

18 Inner London Education Authority *The Junior School Project: A Summary of the Main Findings*, London, ILEA, 1986.

19 HMI *The Teaching and Learning of Reading in Primary Schools 1991*, London, DES, 1992, p. 11. See also HMI *The Teaching and Learning of Reading in Primary Schools*, London, DES, 1991, p. 12.

20 Many books discuss home/school relations in the context of reading. For example, *A Framework for Reading: Creating a Policy in the Primary School* (ref. 14 above) makes nearly forty suggestions of ways in which parents can be involved in reading and literacy activities. A good but highly structured handbook is Branston, P. and Provis, M. *Children and Parents Enjoying Reading*, London, Hodder & Stoughton, 1986.

CHILDREN'S BOOKS

ASHLEY, BERNARD, *All My Men*, Puffin.

HOFFMAN, MARY, *Dog Powder*, Heinemann.

LAVELLE, SHEILA, *My Best Fiend*, Young Lions.

4

Fiction in the Classroom

In the first chapter I suggested in general terms how fiction can work, and implied some purposes for its use in the primary classroom. The thrust of that discussion was, in part, that the experience of fiction can be of value in a range of different contexts, that written stories have a variety of functions, and therefore that fiction should be considered by primary teachers as much more than just raw material with which to practise decoding print. But the long-term and rather insubstantial goals discussed so far need now to be translated into short-term objectives and activities for classroom use.

To start with it may be as well to bear in mind some more of the factors which Raleigh suggests[1] contribute to the formation of reluctant readers in the secondary school, to add to those discussed earlier in the context of school policies. He maintains that a disproportionate number of children who end up resisting reading were initiated into it by methods which highlighted the techniques rather than the functions of reading, and which communicated a narrow sense of what reading is and what it's good for; that in such children's primary schools there tended to be a heavy emphasis on reading aloud to the teacher from reading scheme books and little opportunity for extended silent reading from self-chosen material. Partly as a result, Raleigh suggests, such children have failed to develop their own reliable criteria for choosing books, tend to make bad choices, and so do not develop a sense of themselves as readers.

A range of questions arises as soon as we start to think about how such problems can be addressed. Is it possible in practice to incorporate work with fiction into the classroom in ways which will develop children's broader competences in language and literacy? How can fiction be used in ways which contribute to children's personal, social and intellectual development? What types of lessons and classroom activities may contribute towards achieving such goals? How should teachers' and children's work with a novel or a story take shape, and how should it progress?

Such questions require the elaboration (in this and the next chapter) of strategies for using fiction: activities and methods in this area of the curriculum, as in any other, are most likely to be productive and useful if they are based on a clear and well-thought-out rationale linked to achieving long-term goals. But such a strategy must also be closely related to and focused on the everyday practicalities of classrooms, thus creating an appropriate compromise between what is ideally desirable and what is pragmatically achievable. We need therefore to consider several issues which will contribute to the construction of a positive, yet realistic, programme for children.

Books for children

The 1990 version of the National Curriculum programme of study for Key Stage 2 states: 'Pupils should read an increasingly wide range and variety of texts in order to become more experienced readers. They should be encouraged to develop their personal taste in reading with guidance from the teacher and to become more independent and reflective.'[2] Not surprisingly, according to HMI: 'The teachers of classes achieving high standards generally ensured that the children had a wide variety of good reading material'.[3] Some ways in which a wide variety of books can be introduced to a wide variety of children can be discussed in a moment, but a more contentious question needs to be considered first: how can we define what reading material is good? The criteria suggested in Chapter 3 may be helpful in making such judgements, but the question deserves a little further consideration.

GOOD BOOKS?

A very large number of writers have attempted to establish criteria for assessing the quality of children's books, but such attempts have sometimes been unprofitably derived from academic criticism of the great works of English Literature, sometimes they have been mutually contradictory, occasionally impossibly restrictive, and quite often they have been based on a very limited view of the ways in which children's fiction can work and the uses to which it can be put. Just one, very well-known example is C. S. Lewis's magisterial comment that: 'No book is really worth reading at the age of ten which is not equally (and often far more) worth reading at the age of fifty'.[4] This is surely nonsense. Some of the books children read are often regarded by adults as banal rubbish, yet even they may play a valuable part in the process of reading development. For example, the experience of 12-year-old Karnail, like many other children, had always been that 'the books resisted him'. But as Donald Fry relates, it was Enid Blyton's *Well Done, Secret Seven* that for the first time made reading easy and made him feel like a real reader.[5]

My own inclination then, up to a point, is to be as eclectic as possible. One reason is that books often work in unpredictable and mysterious ways that cannot be measured, and so any adult judgement that a specific book will in some way be good or bad for children is likely to be at best idiosyncratic and at worst very fallible. But also for another reason: one of our most pressing problems in primary schools is to persuade all our children that reading something – anything – is in itself a worthwhile activity. Faced with children like Karnail, and there are very many like him, we are much more likely to have to find ways of making reading as attractive as possible than having time or enthusiasm for fine discriminations of literary merit between, say, *Conrad's War* and *Carrie's War*. At the point when children are reading voraciously, but more or less indiscriminately, it may be appropriate to be concerned with criteria which enable judgements to be made about the literary quality of the books, but probably not much before then. Most of the time, for children to read material that to an adult's eye appears to be rather mediocre, if not actually rubbish, is surely better than reading nothing at all.[6]

This is not meant to imply, of course, that the teacher should simply abdicate responsibility for her children's reading choices. Rather, it is to propose that the teacher's role is to guide, to suggest and to lead, but not to impose too forcefully an adult view of what is appropriate or good. Above all patience is needed. Even if attempts to extend the range of children's reading fail at first, it's worth remembering that they do emerge from such experience eventually, often as stronger and more purposeful readers. As long as children are reading something there is at least the possibility of widening their range sooner or later, but too much pressure too early may lead eventually to children abandoning reading for pleasure, in which case they may be lost for good.

DIFFICULT BOOKS?

A related issue is the view taken by many teachers in primary schools, and implicit in the most recent National Curriculum proposals, that children should be presented with reading material of increasing difficulty and challenge. It's hard to disagree with this in principle, since clearly one of the main reasons why children are in school is to learn, which implies gradual exposure to more complex ideas, concepts, knowledge and indeed language. But on the other hand, if after every successful reading experience the child is rewarded only by something more demanding, and is only allowed to pause at a level when he or she is having difficulties coping with it, the pleasure and fun of reading stories is likely to evaporate. If such painful experiences are repeated very often the child may eventually become one of those readers who can but doesn't. Similarly, if the teacher with commendable enthusiasm for the classics of children's literature recommends books whose style and language is beyond the child's capabilities, the results may be negative, as with Susan in one of Terry Pratchett's novels: "Susan hated Literature. She'd much prefer to read a good book".[7]

It's perhaps worth bearing in mind that adults who read fluently and widely do not always choose books which are at the limits of their ability to read and understand, although they may occasionally do so. Nor having finished a conceptually complex and structurally challenging book do adults necessarily look for something even more formidable – 'Now I've finished reading Piaget I can start on Wittgenstein!'. Rather, having to read harder and harder books would almost certainly turn most of us off reading, and so most skilled adult readers often choose stories which are light, undemanding and attractive, which fit a mood or an occasion, and which can be effortlessly enjoyed. For the same reasons, then, we cannot reasonably expect children always to read at the limits of their ability. They too need the easy books and the pleasure of finishing a story quickly and easily.

For these reasons there needs to be a balance between confirming and reinforcing children's existing sense of themselves as readers by providing them with material which is exciting and rewarding yet simple and easy to read, and the need to provide access to more complex and demanding material in order to extend and further develop children's attainments. The right book in the right place at the right time is a fine balance to strike, but one that teachers need to aim for.

The classroom context

Providing children with a worthwhile experience of fiction requires an appropriate classroom environment. Ideally, the classroom should contain a plentiful selection of attractive books in a separate book area which is both accessible and comfortable for children to read in. The financial constraints on schools often make the former an aspiration rather than a reality, and the physical characteristics of many classrooms often make the latter very difficult if not impossible. However, in most situations it is possible to provide at least a small quiet area for reading. This may consist only of a few books in a corner of the classroom marked off by bookshelves, and enclosing an area of carpet with a few old cushions, but it's a start. Even such a very basic book corner indicates to children that this part of the classroom is special, that it's not for talking or playing, or even for writing or doing other school activities, but just for reading, because quiet reading is regarded as really important. Of course, given a bit more space and money, – more ambitious reading and browsing areas are possible with proper room dividers, modern bookshelves and book boxes, comfortable chairs, and so on. Such book corners are common in early years classrooms, but less often provided for older children. Yet their needs for appropriate space for reading are just as great.

The books in classroom collections need some organization and management, although in a much simpler and more informal way than is appropriate for school libraries. However small the collection of books may be, they need to be attractively arranged and looked after so that they appear inviting and interesting as well as being easily accessible. If possible, the books available need to change fairly frequently so that the collection continues to look fresh and interesting, perhaps by regularly distributing different books from the school library. And an occasional display of books that are new or special in some way, or connected to a theme of current classroom interest, can encourage children to pick up a book and start to read.

Some teachers group classroom books by topic so that children can easily pursue a particular interest, others shelve books alphabetically by author in order to provide experience of the way proper libraries are organized and to provide opportunities to practise alphabetical indexing, and yet others group books according to reading difficulty. Each of these methods has advantages and disadvantages. For example, coding books by level of reading difficulty has the advantage of guiding children towards books that they are likely to be able to cope with, but on the other hand it can lead to an unhelpful competitiveness among children, whereby the difficulty of the text becomes more important than its quality or interest. Grouping books by topic has the obvious advantage that it locates together books of a particular type, but it makes it more difficult for children to find another book by a particular author whose stories they enjoy. So whichever method is used, either singly or in combination, it should be as part of a flexible system so that children are provided with a helpful framework rather than a straitjacket which constrains choice too much. It is important too that the children fully understand the system in use and, once again, that they are involved as much as possible in putting it into practice, such as by helping to make decisions about what books are displayed, and how, or by taking responsibility for the routine maintenance of the area.

Although physical resources are important for classroom work, the most significant resource in the classroom, as in the school as a whole, is the teacher. Above all else, her enthusiasm for and knowledge of books is contagious, and probably more than any other factor this determines whether or not children's experience of fiction is productive. Very often a teacher's recommendation can make all the difference to a child's reading, and so while teachers are not required to see themselves as unpaid agents of the publishing industry, a little of the zeal of the salesman does not go amiss. There is an often-quoted story of the writer Edward Blishen, who was taught by 'an Irishman appointed to teach mathematics on the grounds that he was an international lawn tennis player'. Although Blishen learnt little mathematics, his teacher's idiosyncratic enthusiasm for literature, his habit of discussing books with passionate joy – or sometimes scorn – and his eccentric methods of encouraging the boys in his class to read made a lasting impression: 'How influential to have this utterly natural exhibition by a grown-up, with whom you were constantly in contact, of the quality of a true reader who displayed before us, quite naturally, all the responses to books, rage as well as deep appreciation.'[8] The basic point, then, is that the teacher needs to know and enjoy books in order that her encouragement of children's reading is based on a genuine commitment and not empty exhortation. This necessarily implies some reading of children's books. Teachers who have not kept in contact with recent fiction for children will find that the quality of the best books is extraordinarily high in comparison with most adult fiction. (Perhaps it's because writers for children cannot rely on sex and violence to sell their books that in order to attract and hold the attention of a fickle audience they have to be masters of storytelling!) The best children's books can certainly be read and enjoyed by adults because they are well written and because they have a multi-layered quality: they can be enjoyed at different levels. The adult reader of the work of writers as varied as Anthony Browne, Jan Mark or Alan Garner, for example, will appreciate the depth and subtlety of their stories, even though children may simply enjoy them as exciting narratives with strong and attractive characters. Interestingly, Anne Fine's wonderfully comic children's novel *Goggle-Eyes* was recently televised in a production aimed at adults, presumably because it was regarded as being dramatically strong enough to entertain adults as well as children – which it certainly did.

Many teachers, however, do not need convincing of the value of reading children's books, but simply find that the ever-increasing demands of teaching make time for thoughtful and concentrated reading of any kind very difficult to find. There's no complete solution to this, in the sense that reading children's books does indeed take time, but setting a regular but realistic target may be helpful. For example, it might be possible for a teacher to say that she will read a children's book over one weekend each month, or several during a specific time in the summer holidays. Once again, it's particularly valuable to find a friend or colleague who shares the interest because mutual support and the possibility of sharing makes the whole process so much easier. In some areas, groups of teachers from different schools – and librarians and interested parents too – occasionally meet to discuss books, which is even better: not only is it worthwhile in itself, but it provides a powerful incentive to read before and after meetings. Appendix 1 (pp. 130–8) provides some suggestions of specific titles which teachers may find helpful for these purposes; alternatively, there are several books of extracts from a variety of children's books which can provide teachers with an easily accessible flavour of what is available.[9]

Presenting fiction to children

Given enthusiastic and knowledgeable teachers working in reasonably good physical conditions and with access to decent resources, a variety of productive encounters between children and stories are possible.

HEARING STORIES

The first and foremost means of enabling children to gain positive contacts with fiction is to provide them with the experience of listening to stories of all kinds: as we have seen, the National Curriculum requirements demand it.

It is almost impossible to over-emphasize the value of this activity for children of any age or reading level.

By listening, children can understand and appreciate stories that are beyond their ability to read themselves. If the teacher chooses a story which is attractive and appealing, children can gain much from even a quite complex text and can thus be introduced to themes and topics and styles of writing which would otherwise be inaccessible. Introducing children to texts which they cannot yet read is also very useful because the more we know about a job beforehand, the easier it is to do eventually; as Aidan Chambers has observed: 'listening to books read aloud prepares us for what we may find, and what we should look out for, as we perform the more difficult task of reading print for ourselves'.[10] Similarly, children can get a greater sense of the range and variety of what is available by hearing well-chosen stories, can discover that there are many interesting and exciting books that are quite different from those they currently read – and very often children will respond to a story of a different style or genre by asking to read it themselves.

Listening to stories is thus a crucial aspect of learning about and learning from fiction, as well as providing the pleasure of a collaborative experience in which all children, whatever their abilities in reading or lack of them, can share equally. It is in a sense the most natural way of discovering the rhythm and music of words, how they can be used to create, describe and imply secondary worlds, and how they can engender emotions of wonder, excitement, happiness or sadness. In other words, listening enables children to gain easy access to meaning, without the necessity of attending to the decoding of text. In addition, through hearing stories children can begin to understand how stories work, how they have beginnings, middles and ends, how characters, settings and plots are organized, and they can absorb important lessons about the structure of language and how it can be used in a variety of different discourses, all of which is of great value for children's individual reading – and, indirectly, writing.

Many children do not hear stories read fluently and expressively by the teacher nearly enough. In some classrooms it occurs quite rarely and is used essentially as a tactic to calm the children down, a period of quiet relaxation before children go out to the playground or go home after the exertions of the day. This is an understandable motive and there's nothing really wrong with it, but if it is the only reason for using fiction, and the only time children hear an adult reading a story really well, the experience is somewhat marginalized. But if, on the other hand, children regularly hear a variety of stories, carefully chosen and well read, the effects on the quality and quantity of children's individual reading, and the sum total of their experience of fiction in the classroom can be substantial.

For reading aloud to work well, it needs to be planned. First of all, it's helpful to think in terms of a range and mix of texts which can provide children with an appropriately broad and varied experience over the course of a term or so. For example, a sequence of short stories might be read, perhaps linked together by author or theme, each of which could be completed in one session. This could be followed by a longer and more complex novel, read serially over a couple of weeks, followed in turn by a picture-book or two, and concluding with a re-reading of a book which the children are familiar with and is generally a class favourite. Occasionally the teacher might read just the first chapter or two of a book and invite children who have enjoyed the story so far to continue individually or as a group. Good picture-books are particularly valuable for small to medium-sized groups, and not only for younger children, partly because they are usually short and easily accessible, and partly because they are in a sense audiovisual: the listener has work to do with his eyes as well as with his ears in order to make sense of the text.

When selecting specific texts it is worth choosing a variety of stories: some which are more subtle and difficult than those the children are used to, some that involve topics that children don't usually choose for themselves, others that deal with familiar themes in a fresh and challenging way, and, of course, some that are amusing and easy and just fun to read and to listen to. However, not all stories read aloud successfully. Many novels are just too long even for serialization, others don't really work well aloud – *Watership Down*, for example, in my experience suffers from both problems – and many others need a lot of editing. Only by trying out different stories is it possible to discover what really works with a particular group of children and what they respond to well, although experience suggests that one is rarely able to please all the people all the time![11]

The organization of read-aloud sessions similarly needs a little thought. Story reading needs to be regular, but the timing will obviously depend on local circumstances, the age of the children, and on the nature of the book to be read. Little and often is probably a good rule of thumb, especially for younger children, but a more complex novel, read to an older age group, may benefit from less frequent but longer sessions, although in my experience twenty minutes or so is about as long as most children can be expected to listen intently. It's best to ensure that children are sitting comfortably and, especially if reading a picture-book, that they can easily see the reader – and she can see them. If the size of the audience can vary – small group, large group, whole class – so much the better. It's also useful to have more than one copy of the text available, and ideally several, since reading aloud so often encourages children to want to try to read the story, or something very similar, for themselves.

Preparing and practising the reading is also necessary: a few teachers are effortlessly good at reading to children, but generally it's not quite as easy as it looks. Even if the story is one that is very well known, it's actually rather difficult to read aloud well without at least looking over the text beforehand and, preferably, trying it out aloud. The actual classroom reading may usefully be prefaced with a brief recapitulation of the story so far, or, if the text is a new one, a short discussion of author, title and front cover picture, and of predictions and expectations of what the book may be about. During the reading children may wish to respond or comment, or the teacher may feel the need to stop and explain or ask questions. Usually it's better, as far as possible, to postpone such discussion until after the reading, since otherwise the flow and continuity of the story can be lost, particularly if, as often happens, the talk begins to move away from the story towards other relevant but different issues. After the reading, certainly, some discussion will arise; this may very often be quite casual and brief, a few questions by the teacher, any necessary explanation of puzzling ideas or vocabulary, mutual expressions of appreciation of the story. Sometimes, however, the teacher may wish to organize discussion in a more structured and formal way, or move into other related classroom activities; some suggestions of appropriate strategies are provided in Chapter 5.

As with any other skill, practice improves performance. All teachers can read stories well if they are willing to devote some time and attention to acquiring and practising the skills involved; as always, time and energy may be in short supply, but it does make a real difference to children's experience of literature.

TELLING STORIES

If some children hear stories read infrequently, listening to a story that is told is even less common. This is unfortunate, because the experience of hearing a story told by a skilled storyteller has a unique ambience and impact. The intimacy and sense of taking part in an activity which is part performance, part conversation, has a peculiar magic.

We all, adults and children alike, know lots of stories; we all tell stories all the time. Every time we tell a joke, pass on some gossip, provide an account of an event or recount an anecdote, we are telling each other stories. What is more, teachers all know lots of stories for children: it would be very difficult to talk to a class without doing so. By the upper end of the primary school, many of the stories we tell children are in the form of explanation – of the water cycle, of number bases, or whatever – but we also know fictional stories: most adults could make a reasonable stab at *Noah*, or *Jack and the Beanstalk*, or *The Boy Who Cried Wolf*, or *The Christmas Story*, or *Robin Hood*, and probably many others of a similar kind, more or less from memory. With a little practice, all teachers could learn to tell a range of stories fluently and effectively. But generally after children have reached the age of 7 or 8, for some reason it is assumed that storytelling is no longer of sufficient importance to make time for. In fact it is very valuable, partly because it has the same beneficial effects as hearing stories read, but also because it is such an enjoyable and natural activity in its own right.

Stories can be told in a variety of different ways, and most teachers adopt techniques and approaches that best fit their own personal style and the tastes of the children, more or less by trial and error. Nevertheless, a few suggestions may be helpful. First, the quality of the story is central. If it's really good children will often respond well, even if the performance is indifferent, but the reverse is not generally true. This means choosing a story which the storyteller herself likes and enjoys, which has a simple basic structure, and one that is fairly sure to fit the age and characteristics of the audience. Myths, legends and folk-tales are a good place to start: one of the reasons they have stood the test of time and are still enjoyed today is that they have a clear theme, an unambiguous point, and are usually written in accessible language, which helps to make them easy for the storyteller to learn and for the audience to understand and to remember. Stories that are long or complex, or have many characters, are not usually suitable for telling. Second it's important for the storyteller to learn thoroughly the outline of the story, so that she can confidently improvise around it, sure of where the climax is, when it's best to pause for effect, what parts are funny or sad, and so on. On the other hand, most skilled storytellers do not try to memorize the whole text word for word in the way an actor does, except for a few sentences at the beginning: 'Once upon a time. . .', 'Long, long ago. . .'; and ending, '. . . so they all lived happily ever after', '. . . and what became of them nobody knows' – and perhaps a few crucial phrases – 'little pig, little pig, let me come in'. To learn the whole story off by heart is both difficult and time-consuming, and also tends to dilute the spontaneity of a performance – and, in my experience, if one forgets a bit in the middle there is a tendency to come to a juddering halt! Third, storytelling is a form of drama, in a way that reading a story isn't. It's just you and the audience without the mediating text. This is not the place for a lengthy discussion of the techniques of dramatic performance, but clearly audibility and volume, expression and tones of voice, pace, gesture, eye contact, and so on are even more important than when reading aloud, and need to be thought about and preferably practised beforehand.

And finally, it's not only the teacher who can read or tell stories. It's sometimes possible to persuade adults other than the teacher to read a story to a group, or to the class – parents, other teachers, the headteacher, visitors to the school, and so on. Such readings naturally provide a different choice of stories, another style of reading, and thus a variety of experience. The same is true for storytelling; a variety of adults can be involved – and it may even be possible in some areas to make use of the extraordinary talents of a professional storyteller. Children too tell stories of all kinds, all the time, to their friends and often to their parents, and they too can be encouraged to re-tell stories they have read or heard, or tell their own made-up stories, either to a small group or to the whole class. Children, as well as adults, learn a lot about the nature of stories by telling them.[12]

AUDIOVISUAL STORIES

Fiction can also be presented to children audiovisually. Film or video versions, or computer-based story adventures, can all provide an extra dimension to the experience of stories. The disadvantage of such audiovisual stories, of course, is that they are expensive to buy, even though they are often well worth the money. Audiotaped stories, on the other hand, either home-made or professionally produced, are just as worthwhile and practical, and much cheaper. Provided a tape recorder and some headphones are available, children can then listen to a story while following the text at the back of the classroom or in another convenient corner, without disturbing other children. Taped stories lack the immediacy and visual impact of a live performance and in general are no substitute for hearing stories read by the teacher, but they can be a very useful additional resource. If, for example, a child wants to hear a favourite story several times, or the teacher wants to add to the stock of stories which children know, or even if there are just odd moments in the school day when a group of children has finished other work, taped stories can profitably be used. They are excellent for the development of both listening and reading skills, and make an activity which is very popular with children in many classrooms.

Children reading

Listening to stories is crucial, but it is not enough. Children need also to read by themselves in order to practise their developing skills, and also so that they can engage with a variety and range of stories and texts which match their own individual needs and interests.

SILENT READING

One of the most difficult problems in classrooms is finding time for individual children to have access to books, and time to read. This is not easy and never has been, but has become even harder in recent years as the demands of the curriculum on teachers and children have relentlessly increased, and there is so much to do, so much that has to be got through. But if we are serious about the value of fiction we have to make the provision of time for silent reading a high priority.

In some classrooms such quiet reading is relatively neglected. This may of course partly be due to pressures of time, but it may also be due to the teacher's slightly guilty feeling that children really ought to be doing something, producing something tangible, rather than just sitting reading. Most classroom activities, whatever their real value, result in an end-product: a piece of writing, a page of sums, which provides evidence that the children have been working, and by implication evidence also that the teacher has been doing her job. Quiet reading is unsatisfactory from this point of view, since it does not necessarily have a physical end-product. Unfortunately this leads some teachers either to reduce the times for individual reading or to insist that every reading is followed by an activity designed to produce evidence that something has been achieved, which can, if necessary, be shown to the headteacher or to parents. It's not easy to prove, but just as with listening to stories it needs to be asserted that books work in mysterious and subtle, as well as obvious and tangible ways, and that the experience of reading a book of one's own choice for a prolonged period is of just as much, if not greater, value in the long term than other classroom activities which appear to be more immediately productive. And once again, the benefit is likely to be greatest for those children who come from homes where quiet reading is not part of everyday family routine.

Some schools have introduced a system, variously entitled but most commonly known as USSR (Uninterrupted Sustained Silent Reading), by which quiet reading is timetabled for a period each day, perhaps just before or just after one of the natural breaks in the school day. During this time all the children and the teacher, and in some cases other adults in the school, read a book from school or from home of their own choice.[13] The first three words in the acronym are all important: the reading needs to be uninterrupted by the teacher or by children doing other tasks, sustained for a period of time varying between 10 and 30 minutes a day, depending on the age and concentration span of the children, and silent in that while there are times to discuss and talk about what we are reading, this is not one of them, and quiet should therefore prevail. USSR is a very valuable technique, since it is helpful in developing a sense that reading is something everyone does, that it is a beneficial and enjoyable habit, that choosing for oneself and reading at one's own pace are attractive features of reading, and because the teacher's own participation demonstrates to the children that it is an activity to be taken seriously.

Alternatively, or preferably in addition to USSR, encouraging silent reading means finding time for children to read individually, and not only or most frequently in odd moments when children have finished their other classroom assignments. Reading is too important to give children the impression that it can be fitted in only if there is time after the real work has been completed, and all too often it's the slower learning children, who really need the reading experience, who never do get the time to do it because they're still struggling to finish their other work. If possible, it's much better if a time can be scheduled for each child to read quietly as one of the essential tasks to complete during the school day. This has the added advantage of being rather more flexible than whole-class USSR-type reading sessions, in that the length of time can vary from day to day according to the child's interest and involvement, where he has got to in the story, and what other work he has to do. A possible disadvantage is that it is rather more difficult for the teacher to keep track of where each child has got to in their reading, but if combined with some whole-class reading sessions this is not difficult to overcome.

READING ALOUD

The practice of asking children to follow a text while it is read round the whole class is fortunately rare nowadays: unskilled readers hated to have their incompetence so publicly exposed, while children who could read well were bored, irritated and held back by the hesitant and stumbling reading of others. Such multiple unprepared reading must also be one of the surest ways of destroying the meaning and flow of a story and the possibility of characterization. But on the other hand, it is valuable for children to gain some experience of the skills of reading aloud well, and so to provide opportunities for children to choose a favourite story, practise reading out loud, and then read to other children in the class or to one or more younger or less skilled readers, or even for an audience of parents, is very worthwhile. Alternatively, a group of children could collect a series of short extracts on a common theme and practise a reading, or could use a story that has plenty of dialogue to prepare a dramatized reading of the text, with each individual taking a narrator's or character's role. In each case it is possible for children to perform live or to record their performance on to tape for other children to listen to. All such activities are very beneficial both for the readers and for the listeners.

Asking children to read aloud to the teacher is very common in most primary classrooms and many teachers regard it as a central feature of the way they organize reading in the classroom. It is undoubtedly of value for all children, especially, but not only, those who are struggling, and is indeed often a necessity in order for the teacher to assess how children's reading is progressing. However, it is no substitute for frequent silent reading, since skilled and fluent adults normally read silently and – apart from teachers reading to children – read aloud rather rarely in every-day life.

There is evidence that listening to fewer children reading, but for longer periods, is more productive than trying to hear large numbers of children read almost every day, since this inevitably results in a rushed and unsatisfactory experience for the reader – and probably a headache for the teacher![14] Certainly the experience of reading aloud to the teacher a page or two torn out of context from a reading scheme book in, from the child's point of view, the atmosphere of a test is not one which is conducive to the improvement of reading skill, let alone the appreciation of literature. If it is possible to listen to children for a more extended period, and if it can be viewed as an enjoyable sharing of the story accompanied and followed by discussion of its contents and implications, rather than essentially as an assessment in which every minor error is noted and corrected, the experience is likely to be much more productive.

Generally, the teacher's role, when hearing a child read, should be one of support and encouragement, reinforcement of the strategies he or she already uses – as all readers do – to read for meaning, and sharing enjoyment and appreciation of the story. Usually it is only when the child gets quite confused, or stops completely, or loses the sense of the passage, that more direct intervention is needed. It may be, of course, if this happens frequently, that the book is just too difficult and needs to be replaced by something more accessible. But if the story is generally of about the right level, it is often helpful to go back a little and try again, or to read on further and come back to the puzzling word or sentence subsequently, thus using, as far as possible, the clues provided by the context. Occasionally it may be necessary to look directly at the problem word or phrase and try to work out what it means.[15]

As children's reading develops it may be useful to lay as much or more stress on discussion of the implications of the text rather than on decoding. By talking with the child about the author's intentions, the characterization, the language, the structure of the story, its relationship to real life, and so on, the reader can begin to acquire the more sophisticated reading skills of the fluent adult reader. But to repeat, however the interaction is managed the most significant aspect of reading to and with the teacher is that the child feels encouraged and positive about the experience. Only thus is he or she likely to move a little further towards becoming a committed reader.

A number of alternative strategies, commonly known as shared, paired or group reading, have been developed which may also be helpful. The details of these vary, but essentially they involve children taking turns to read aloud and to listen, either in a partnership with one other child, or in a small group of children. In each case a teacher or other adult – usually a parent – may also participate. Each child takes it in turn to read aloud and to listen to his partner or to another member of the group. This can be very productive, since it permits the collaborative and enjoyable sharing of the story, provides more experience of listening to and talking about stories, and provides children with an opportunity to practise their reading skills. If the teacher occasionally joins in, she will be able to participate in discussion and stimulate children's responses with appropriately challenging questions, and also can monitor and assess reading behaviour in a different context. It is best to keep the groups small; four is probably preferable if the group is unsupervised, five or at the most six if an adult is to be a member. The composition of the group may vary from time to time: children of about the same reading ability, friendship groups, mixed ability groups, even mixed age groups, all have some advantages, but friendship groups may work best at first. They will obviously need several copies of the text (or one copy of a 'big book'[16] may suffice) and initially this should be short, simple and fairly certain to be enjoyed, although as children become familiar with the activity they may increasingly make choices about the text they would like to read or re-read. Like any other worthwhile classroom work, group reading sessions need careful organization at first, but children learn the procedures and conventions quite quickly, and soon begin to negotiate and manage group relationships for themselves. Learning to co-operate is useful experience for children, and group reading has the additional merit that it reduces the pressure on the teacher to hear all the children read quite so frequently, because they are at least getting some alternative form of support. It also creates valuable time for the teacher to concentrate on giving individual help to those children who really need it.[17]

Advertising stories

The suggestions so far have recommended direct means of presenting stories, and ways of providing children with opportunities to read for themselves, in the context of the types of everyday classroom work familiar to most primary teachers. But there are several other approaches to developing children's understanding and appreciation of fiction which are less common in schools but nevertheless worth considering. To spend a little classroom time teaching simple book skills, for example, is very useful, because the more knowledge-able children are about books the better: one of the reasons some children are slightly apprehensive and uncertain about reading is because they have never, as it were, made friends with books. As Anne Baker has observed in a comment which is relevant to the use of fiction and to other areas of reading development, 'As children come to appreciate how books work, their power to use them grows'.[18] One very skilful teacher I know occasionally holds what she calls a 'book talk' session, in which for a few minutes she will talk about a children's book, making sure that there are copies available to satisfy the subsequent demand to read it. She says a little about the kind of book it is, how the story begins, perhaps reads a paragraph or two, tells the children anything she knows about the author, draws attention to the illustrator and publisher, and says why she likes the book or what is particularly attractive about it. She then invites the children to make a comment or two about any story they have read and enjoyed recently. In addition, this teacher operates another simple system for promoting books: children are permitted to stick coloured stars on to the spines of books they have read and wish particularly to recommend, and she will occasionally draw children's attention to what their peers have enjoyed. In such ways she introduces children and books to each other in an easy and natural way.

Another equally simple possibility is to designate an area of the classroom wall as a book notice-board, on which teacher or children put anything relevant: reviews written by children or cut out from magazines, publishers' publicity posters, illustrations of any kind, designs for book covers, photo-graphs of authors, appropriately decorated short passages – jokes, poems – from a book, and so on. Children are often very enthusiastic about this and the space rapidly fills up, so old material needs to be removed, perhaps to a scrapbook or to a folder of cuttings that children can look at if they wish to, or even for a selection to be reprinted in a class magazine.

Yet another particularly valuable activity is to arrange – or allow children to arrange – time and space for an extracurricular book-reading club. Not all children will want to be involved, but the enthusiastic and committed book readers tend to pull others in with them. With guidance from the teacher, children can read and discuss books together and perhaps construct a simple programme of book-related activities: looking after the book notice-board, assisting with library routines, inviting speakers to come and talk, writing letters to favourite authors, exploring catalogues for new books to buy for the school, investigating what stories are available on a particular theme of interest and producing an illustrated bibliography, and so on, almost indefinitely. Not only is such work useful in terms of extending the range and variety of children's reading, but it also makes reading a social activity, one through which children can gain a real sense of community and co-operation because they are working together on a shared interest.

Matching children with books

The quantity and diversity of fiction available for children is almost infinite. At the same time children are complicated and idiosyncratic individuals who vary in their preferences for books in ways that are often eccentric and unpredictable. And, furthermore, what children like can change with bewildering speed; the serialization of a book on television, or a popular film, for example, can create instant acclaim; and sometimes a problem if the text of the original book is much too difficult for children to read, however highly motivated they have become from viewing the story. Matching child and book is thus very challenging, but is also central to the task of enabling children to become increasingly fluent and committed readers.

There are, first of all, several strategies which are worth considering for use with all or any children, whatever their age or stage of development. The more the teacher knows the children, their interests, enthusiasms, likes and dislikes, their knowledge and experience, the more likely it is that she can make a sensible suggestion of what book or what kinds of book each individual would be most likely to enjoy. Similarly, the teacher's awareness of what the child has read and enjoyed before, his reading and writing ability, and the degree to which he is willing and able to tackle new ideas and themes, can all provide helpful clues. To some extent, then, the teacher is likely to be able to make informed guesses about appropriate reading matter simply through her everyday knowledge of the children. But there are a number of ways of extending and focusing this ordinary familiarity. Observing what kinds of books a child most often, and which he rarely or never, chooses from the class or school library can be helpful, as can listening to what children say in informal conversations with each other. But most of all, talking to children about books is central to making a match between them. The answers to even very simple questions can be informative. For example:

- What sort of stories do you like best?
- What is the best book you have ever read?
- What books do you have at home that you particularly like?
- What was the last book you read? Did you like it?
- Are there any books that you have read more than once?

Such questions and answers can provide opportunities for the teacher to make appropriate suggestions, such as:

- Why don't you try. . .
- If you liked that, you'll enjoy this. . .
- This is a story about a girl who's rather like you. . .
- Why don't you look for another book by Dick King-Smith, he's written lots more animal stories. . .
- There are several more books about the Bagthorpes in the library. . .
- This is something rather different but I think you'll find it interesting. . .

It's often possible to use other children's reading experience in rather similar ways. Over the course of a school year and in an average class, the children are likely to read a large number of different titles. Another child's recommendation can often be powerfully motivating. If, therefore, a child has expressed an interest in stories set in schools, for example, it's very helpful to be able to suggest that he or she consults another child who has enjoyed the work of authors like Gene Kemp or Bernard Ashley.

While all such guidance and forms of matching activities are often helpful to children, simply providing opportunities for children to browse is invaluable. As adults, our choices of books to read are sometimes informed by what we have read and enjoyed before, or the recommendation of friends or relations, but often we find new books and authors just by browsing through library or bookshop shelves. And stories we discover for ourselves often seem more attractive than those we are advised or told we ought to read. Just the same is true, if not more so, for inexperienced readers, for whom browsing provides an opportunity to learn more about the kinds of books that are available and might be worth reading. However, one difference between adults and children is that we know how to browse most profitably, how to increase our chances of finding something worth while. For example, we know that we have first to find a section of the library that is likely to hold books we like; that both the front cover picture and a familiar author's name may be helpful, but that neither is an infallible guide; that the 'blurb' is often useful in providing a sense of what the story is about, as is reading the first paragraph or two, or looking at the illustrations if there are any. But children often don't have this kind of awareness, which implies an agenda for the teacher: providing a little time for children to browse individually or with a friend is a start, but most children need some systematic help as well in order to learn to maximize the possibility of finding a book which they will find rewarding.

None of this is intended to suggest, of course, that the teacher should do more at this stage than help children make their own choices; and this means recognizing and accepting that sometimes they will make a wrong choice, as adult readers do too. It is equally a mistake to impose on children the teacher's judgements of what is good and suitable reading as it is to abandon them without any framework within which to make their choices.

If these comments are generally applicable, there are differences between children which also need to be taken into account. Simplifying a lot, in any class in the primary school there are likely to be children who fall into one of three broad categories. First, there are usually some children, if sometimes only a few, who are already enthusiastic and fairly skilful readers of a wide range and variety of fiction, both at home and at school. Second, in most classes there are rather more children who do read fiction occasionally, especially when they are asked or encouraged to do so, but without apparently being particularly excited by or involved in what they read. For such children reading often appears more of a duty than a pleasure, and one that is likely to occur almost entirely in the classroom, rather than at home. Third, there are those children for whom reading is still rather a struggle, and who generally regard it as very hard work. Such children may still be trying hard to achieve a higher level of reading competence, or they may, especially by the age of 10 or 11, be beginning to reject it entirely as an activity whose meaning and purpose is quite impenetrable.

Of course, in practice these neat categories do not always fit precisely. There may well be children whose reading ability is excellent but who prefer information books to fiction, or who invariably choose to read within a very narrow range of stories; or there may be children whose abilities are very limited yet get great pleasure from the very simple stories that they can read. But in general, children who are better at reading tend to be those who are more interested and involved in fiction, and conversely those who find reading difficult are likely to be less committed.

FLUENT READERS

For those children who are already enthusiastic and proficient readers the task is essentially broadening the range of material they encounter and deepening their understanding of what they read. Even the best 10 or 11-year-old readers still have much to learn and much to read and enjoy. It's easy for such children to be relatively neglected since they have already achieved what others are still struggling to come to terms with, but it is important to maintain and develop further their skill and interest. One way of doing so is to enable such children to share their reading experiences with other like-minded children, which is often highly motivating; another is to suggest examples of novels which are as interesting and exciting as their current reading, but which are very different or particularly challenging, thus extending their reading even further.

DEVELOPING READERS

With most children, however, the teacher's task is not so relatively straight-forward, and matching child and book is likely to be a matter of developing different strategies to fit children with a range of characteristics. For example, there are those children who always choose books which are very easy to read, who need to be encouraged to read stories which are just a little more difficult or just a little more varied. Some other children of this age, who are quite good readers, start to move away from fiction to information books; nothing wrong in that, of course, but they may also be encouraged to enjoy stories closely based on fact, or set in realistic contexts. Similarly, in many classes there are those frustrating children who appear to be sunk forever in an ocean of nothing but Enid Blyton or the *Chalet School* series, or, as in my son's case, endless *Dr Who* stories. In such cases, the temptation to insist that the child reads some more literary or worthwhile or more difficult book can be very powerful. But it's actually much more effective to suggest alternatives which are only slightly different from existing reading, perhaps by the same author or dealing with the same themes, and to provide access to a wide variety of other stimulating and exciting books at the right reading and interest levels – my son is now reading stories by authors like Ray Bradbury, Isaac Asimov, Douglas Adams and Terry Pratchett, which is some sort of progress, I suppose!

Children whose reading is less fluent, or occasional rather than committed, provide different and more intractable problems, as one Sheffield teacher discovered:

MISS: (*an enthusiastic and skilled teacher*): Now then Wayne, do you think that nasty Mr Fox will get baby bunny, or will baby bunny reach his burrow in time?

WAYNE: (*an unenthusiastic and unskilled reader*): Miss, I couldn't give a f*** if nasty Mr Fox gets baby rabbit. This book is f***ing boring.[19]

Such children may enjoy a new and intriguing type of fiction they have not met, and found too difficult, before. Short stories, comic strip 'graphic novels,' the brief but plentifully illustrated *Chips and Jessie* books, or one of the series of books recently produced with such children in mind (e.g. *Jets, Banana Books, Superchamps*: see Appendix 1) are particularly valuable here: anything, in other words, except either stories in which the interest level is inappropriate, or books with long dense pages of small print. With some such children even more direct help may be needed: as well as providing texts which are very simply written and directly related to known interests and enthusiasms it may be useful to let such a child listen to a taped version of the story or to read the text to him before he tries to read it for himself. It may also be helpful to share the reading with the child, particularly through the first few pages, to get him into the flow of the story, and to encourage him to retell the story orally during and after reading.

STRUGGLING READERS

Much of this also applies to those children who have not yet fully achieved a fairly minimal level of proficiency, but they are likely to need even more support in their reading. This will certainly include the teacher taking a direct and frequent interest, prompting and encouraging the child, asking his opinion of the story, providing reassurance that progress really is being made, encouraging the child to take books home to read, and so on. But such children need even more than this: it is often the solitary and individual nature of reading, the fact that the reader has to rely entirely on his own limited resources to make sense of the story, that makes reading so difficult. For such children hearing stories is of particular value, and so is talking about what they read with an adult or other children in pairs or a small group, because both activities helpfully make reading a public rather than, or as well as, a private activity. For example, by sharing the jokes, discussing a puzzling or paradoxical passage, considering the implications of an event, relating the story to his or her own experience, exploring the motives and actions of a character, taking account of the ways in which punctuation affects the sense of a passage, and puzzling over new or unfamiliar vocabulary or syntax, texts are made much more accessible. The causes of reading failure are often complex and difficult to solve and the low self-esteem, characteristic of struggling readers, and the avoidance or displacement strategies that often follow, make matters worse. However, by encouraging and participating in constructive activities like these, the teacher can ensure that however limited the child's attainment may be, he or she achieves at least some positive success from his or her reading experience.

Conclusion

Successful teaching and learning with fiction is more likely to take place if the school environment is one consciously designed and managed to provide a facilitating and supportive framework. But in addition, I have suggested in this chapter that a specific policy for work within the classroom is necessary. This classroom policy needs to take account of:

- The physical and human resources available and how they can be used and enhanced.
- Provision for children to hear stories read and told by the teacher, by other adults, or audiovisually.
- A variety of means by which books can be effectively advertised and promoted in the classroom.
- Time within everyday classroom routines for individual reading both aloud and silently.
- Ways of enabling children to choose sensibly, strategies for matching children with books, and methods of supporting children's reading.

As well as providing such tangible forms of support for children's reading, it is also obviously important to think about the quality of their experience of fiction. This will entail some consideration of the interaction of readers with texts, and how children respond to what they read.

References

1 Raleigh, M. 'Independent reading', in *The English Magazine*, no. 10, Autumn 1982, p. 22.
2 Department of Education and Science/Welsh Office *English in the National Curriculum (No. 2)*, London, HMSO, 1990, p. 30.
3 HMI *The Teaching and Learning of Reading in Primary Schools*, London, HMSO, 1991, p. 6.
4 Lewis, C. S. 'On stories', reprinted in Meek, M. *et al.* (eds.) *The Cool Web: The Pattern of Children's Reading*, London, Bodley Head, 1977, p. 85.
5 Fry, D. *Children Talk About Books: Seeing Themselves as Readers*, Milton Keynes, Open University Press, 1985, p. 47.
6 For a development of this argument see Dickinson, P. 'A defence of rubbish', *Children's Literature in Education*, No. 3, 1970.
7 Pratchett, T. *Soul Music*, London, Gollancz, 1994.
8 Blishen, E. 'That's all', in Fox, G. *et al.* (eds.) *Writers, Critics and Children*, London, Heinemann, 1976.
9 For example, Fadiman, C. (ed.) *The Puffin Children's Treasury* Harmondsworth, Penguin, 1985; *The Illustrated Treasury of Modern Literature for Children*, London, Hamlyn, 1985; Webb, K. (ed.) *I Like This Story*, Harmondsworth, Puffin, 1986, and *Meet My Friends*, Harmondsworth, Puffin, 1991.
10 Chambers, A. *The Reading Environment*, Stroud, Thimble Press, 1991, p. 53.
11 Many suitable books for reading aloud are suggested by Trelease, J. *The Read Aloud Handbook*, Harmondsworth, Penguin, 1984.
12 On the value of storytelling in the classroom see Rosen, B. *And None of it Was Nonsense*, London, Mary Glasgow Publications, 1988, and Howe, A. and Johnson, J. *Common Bonds: Storytelling in the Classroom*, Sevenoaks, Hodder & Stoughton, 1992. On techniques of storytelling see the articles in Weir, L. (ed.) *Telling the Tale*, Youth Libraries Group, 1988.
13 For example, Maybin, J. 'Whole-school reading periods', in Hoffman, M. *et al.* (eds.) *Children, Language and Literature*, Milton Keynes, Open University Press, 1983. See also Fenwick, G. *Teaching Children's Literature in the Primary School*, London, David Fulton, 1990, Ch. 4, for a how-to-do-it guide.
14 See Arnold, H. *Listening to Children Reading*, London, Hodder & Stoughton, 1982.
15 Campbell, R. *Hearing Children Read*, London, Routledge, 1988.
16 Such as 'Storytime Giants', published by Oliver & Boyd.
17 See, for example, Bentley, D. and Rowe, A. *Group Reading in the Primary School*, Reading, Reading and Language Information Centre, 1991, and two books of teachers' resources for group reading, Bentley, D. and Reid, D. *Scholastic Literacy Centre: Fiction Blue Set* and *Fiction Red Set*, both Leamington Spa, Scholastic,1993.
18 Baker, A. 'Developing reading with juniors', in Moon, C. (ed.) *Practical Ways to Teach Reading*, London, Ward Lock, 1985, p. 17.

19 Quoted by Gaines, K. 'Teaching literacy and children with special needs', in Beard, R. (ed.) *Teaching Literacy, Balancing Perspectives*, Sevenoaks, Hodder & Stoughton, 1993, p 143.

CHILDREN'S BOOKS

ADAMS, RICHARD, *Watership Down*, Puffin.

BAWDEN, NINA, *Carrie's War*, Puffin.

BLYTON, ENID, *Well Done, Secret Seven*, Knight.

BRENT-DYER, ELINOR, *Chalet School* series, Armada.

CRESSWELL, HELEN, *Bagthorpe* series, Puffin.

DAVIES, ANDREW, *Conrad's War*, Hippo.

DICKS, TERRANCE, *Dr Who* series, Target.

FINE, ANNE, *Goggle-Eyes*, Puffin.

HUGHES, SHIRLEY, *Chips and Jessie*, Young Lions.

Banana Books, Heinemann.

Jets, A. & C. Black, Young Lions.

Superchamps, Heinemann.

5

Readership and Response

Discussing how children read and respond to stories is in one sense very easy, but in a number of others rather difficult. In everyday classroom practice it is usually easy enough to tell whether or not children are reading effectively and enjoying a story because they appear engrossed, they laugh, they want to talk about the story, they are eager for more. Conversely, it is equally easy to tell if a story isn't working: children are easily distracted, seem reluctant to carry on reading, and words like 'boring' begin to be heard. But it is much more difficult to know quite what is going on in children's minds, how the interaction between reader and text gives rise to a response of one kind or another, and how the value of a response can be assessed. However, in an increasingly hard-headed educational world, if we are to argue that reading fiction is of real value to children and not merely light entertainment or an opportunity to practise reading skills, then we need to be able to say something more about the experience than just that the children seemed to have fun. In the context of fiction, happily, enjoyment may often be a corollary of learning, but the teacher's focus has of course to be first and foremost on the latter.

The interaction of readers and texts

For this reason we need first to look in a little detail at what happens when readers read. It is, of course, very difficult to be sure what's going on in a reader's head, since the experience is internal and personal, but several attempts have been made to describe the processes involved, which make at least intuitive sense. Benton and Fox, for example, argue[1] that there are four kinds of mental activity involved in reading fiction, which can help us to understand the ways in which readers construct meaning from a story, and it will be useful to consider their categorization before discussing the implications which arise for the teacher.

PICTURING AND IMAGING

One of the most important ways in which texts work is to enable the reader to construct mental pictures. In other words, as we read we are constantly seeing in our mind's eye what is happening, as if we were actually participating or observing. This is not, of course, either a mechanical or sequential process, as if we were viewing a series of slides. Rather the meaning of the text is constructed from a flux of images in the mind which form and re-form, shift and flow, change and merge, dissolve and evaporate. Eleven-year-old Tracey, for example, reports some of her mental images while reading *One Hundred and One Dalmatians*:

> Like one of the pictures was of the dogs climbing into a house by going through the coal cellar. I could see the back of the van with the flaps down and the dogs jumping in. The van was all dark inside so when the dogs got in I could not see them because they were covered in soot.[2]

Not all readers construct such vivid mental pictures, or do so all the time they are reading – and poor readers do not seem to do it very much at all – but often accomplished readers' responses to stories are essentially visual: indeed, very often readers are disappointed by a film version of a story because the images do not correspond to those in their imagination.

ANTICIPATING AND RETROSPECTING

Anticipation is often a powerful motive for reading, because we want to know both in the short term what happens next, and in the longer term how it is all going to work out in the end. As we read, then, our minds run ahead of the text to try to resolve the questions or ambiguities raised in the story. Detective stories are the most obvious example, since it is largely our attempts to predict the solution to the puzzle which drives us on through the text. But the process occurs to some extent in all stories, and skilled writers use our desire to look ahead to draw us into the story, and then to keep us reading. For example, take the first sentences of two novels for children:

> We'd gone right through the school collecting the teachers' tea money and had got to the canteen door when Danny waved the ten-pound note at me.
>
> (*The Turbulent Term of Tyke Tiler*)

'Where's Papa going with that axe?' said Fern to her mother as they were
setting the table for breakfast

(Charlotte's Web)

In both cases, the writer immediately sets up an incongruity – children in
primary school don't usually have ten-pound notes to wave around, nor do
Dads commonly wield axes at breakfast-time – with the intention that the
reader will want to read on in order to resolve the puzzle. And thus, as
Benton and Fox suggest, we 'engage in a range of predictive activities
including thinking through particular problems "in advance", extrapolating,
hypothesizing, speculating and guessing', or even skipping a few pages to
find out what happens because the tension is unbearable (one avid reader
of detective stories I know routinely reads the last chapter first).

Adult readers also look back, often at the end of a book, again, as in
detective stories, to see how the author skilfully laid clues, traps, diversions
and so on, or, in the case of a more sophisticated fiction, to consider the way
in which the story made its impact and how the author created a believable
secondary world. But we also retrospect as we are actually reading: we make
sense of the text as we go along by adding it to the sum total of what has
gone before, by placing the sentences and paragraphs we are reading into the
context of what we already know. The meanings of each sentence are thus
partly constituted by reflection, by mentally pausing and recollecting, as well
as by hypothesizing and anticipating. For children, being less experienced
readers than adults, it is usually the pull forward of the plot which engages
their interest and enthusiasm, but sensitive teaching can enable them to
understand and enjoy the story more by pausing and reflecting on what has
gone before.

INTERACTING

As we read we do not just picture, predict and retrospect, but to a greater
or lesser degree we become involved, we begin to care about the characters
and what happens to them. Sometimes very powerful emotions can be stirred,
even to the extent of feeling unable to re-read a passage because of the strong
feelings it evokes; for example, Donald Fry quotes one of his interviewees'
reluctance to look at the last page of the textless story *The Snowman* – in which
the eponymous hero melts away to a puddle – because it's so sad.[3] In the same
way for most readers a phrase, a scene, a character from a particular book may
stay with us for years and affect, in some way, our everyday understandings.

But as well as using identification and empathy to help us come to terms with our own lives, we also bring our own experience to bear on a story in order to understand it and make more sense of it. It is this interaction with a text, this interplay between what we know about the physical, social and emotional world, and the interpretation of it presented in a story, that is one of the fundamental ways in which we construct meaning. In other words, reading is not a one-way process of receiving messages from a disembodied speaker; rather, it is a process by which the reader brings his or her experience to the text, and the total effect of reading lies in the interaction of the two. The point is cleverly reinforced by Gene Kemp in her *Charlie Lewis Plays for Time*:

> Mr Carter came round the class to check our work, said mine was satisfactory and asked me to read to him. In a minute he snatched the book off me.
> 'Whatever is this book? Where did you get this?'
> 'It's a follow-up to one we read in class with Mr Merchant, funny and about school, a school like ours.'
> 'I don't care for the tone of it at all. I don't like its language. Leave it. I'll get you a reader.'
> Reader? But I'm the reader. Not the book.

EVALUATING

Finally, both as we read and after we have finished reading we make judgements about the story. As we read we are thinking whether the book is sufficiently appealing and convincing to be worth continuing with or finishing. After we have finished a book we may make an assessment of the experience, leading us to decide that we want to read another book of the same kind or by the ·same author, or alternatively to feel that enough is quite enough. All such thoughts may be entirely private, but often are expressed in the form of appreciative comments to other people, or laughter, or tears – or, conversely, negative remarks about the book or audible groans of disappointment. Sharing our opinions about what we have read – as about anything else – seems to be an activity we engage in naturally as social beings.

The assessments we make of stories vary in their level of sophistication, of course. At the age of 11 I read *Animal Farm* as a delightful farmyard story, but a recent re-reading made me aware of more subtle features of the text! Other books do not really have hidden depths: once you have found out whodunnit in a detective story and admired the author's ingenuity, or come to the neatly resolved climax of an exciting adventure, there isn't often much more to it. But there are also many books, even those for very young children, which provide opportunities for more complex evaluation – the wonderful *Rosie's Walk* is one of the best-known examples. At times too children's evaluations can be quite profound but inarticulately expressed; the fact that children do not have the verbal facility of adults and thus say little more than 'I thought it was great', does not necessarily mean that their response was superficial. Many adult readers can recall a childhood read – *Black Beauty* is a common one – which made a deep impression, even though at the time we could not have said why very eloquently.

Readers and response

If readers' responses are based on these forms of mental activity, singly or, more likely, in complex combination, there are clearly implications for the teacher. First, we need to examine why such responses are of significance, before considering in more detail the teacher's role in encouraging the expression and development of response.

WHY IS RESPONSE IMPORTANT?

To enable children to reflect on what they read, to evaluate it, and to share it, is to make it possible for them to interact with texts more effectively and thus to construct meaning more skilfully, and to learn a little more about themselves and others and the world they live in. Cairney[4] has suggested five reasons why teachers should encourage response, which neatly encapsulate the role of the teacher in this area, and which can be summarized as follows:

• Response is a natural consequence of reading; because reading has social purposes, response often needs to be shared.
• Response allows the reader to re-evaluate the experience of a text: 'as we seek the reactions of others to our meanings, and in turn reflect upon their interpretations, we revise and reshape our own personal text'.
• Response is essential to help build common literary ground: such shared meanings are one of the ways in which we create, maintain and participate in our culture, which in turn shapes our thinking and behaviour.

- Readers learn as a consequence of being party to the responses of others: sharing responses enables the reader to increase his knowledge and understanding of what he has read.
- Response permits the teacher to make judgements and predictions about individual students' reading processes; only through response can the teacher gain evidence of children's learning and progress in reading development.

The teacher's role, therefore, is much more than just encouraging children to read, important though that is. Implicit in Cairney's criteria is the idea that by enabling children to respond to what they read the teacher can play a crucial role in children's social, emotional and intellectual development which extends far beyond the fluent decoding of print.

ENCOURAGING RESPONSE

Encouraging response, I have suggested, is the most important way in which children's experience of fiction can be extended and developed. Unfortunately, however, this is not necessarily easy to do. For a start, children are obviously very varied in any primary classroom, in terms of reading competence, personality, and emotional maturity. This makes it difficult to be sure that classroom work with any particular text will be appropriate for more than a few children at a time. Even if book and child are matched in these terms, the whole thrust of the argument so far has been that there is no one valid interpretation of a story but a multiplicity of personal and often idiosyncratic responses, each of which is unique to the individual and cannot easily be predicted or organized. Stories do not work in straight lines; causes and effects are often blurred, which means that using fiction can seem a rather hit-or-miss affair. Occasionally, too, children's response to a story is somewhat negative, which is rather depressing for the teacher who has introduced a book in the hope and expectation that children will enjoy it. And furthermore, and perhaps of most current concern, there is not always a neat and tidy written product arising from children's responses which can easily be assessed in terms of the discrete categories and levels of the National Curriculum.

One way in which some teachers have been tempted to deal with these genuinely difficult problems is to use fiction largely as a medium for teaching some of the narrower concerns of English and to see response as valid only if it is measurable. Sometimes, for example, passages from children's books are used as raw material for spelling tests or handwriting practice, or for teaching elements of punctuation and grammar, or even more commonly for so-called comprehension tests. To take just one example, in a recently reprinted set of English books for 10-year-olds[5] children are invited to read the first three paragraphs of *Alice in Wonderland*, beginning with: 'Alice was beginning to get very tired of sitting by her sister on the bank, and of having nothing to do; once or twice she had peeped into the book her sister was reading'. The traditional ten questions follow the passage, of which the first three are typical and provide a sense of the demands such work makes: Where was Alice sitting? Who was with her? What was this person doing? It's not difficult to point out the limitations of this sort of exercise, the most obvious of which is that the questions do not actually require children to understand – or even thoroughly read – the text at all; the questions can easily be answered by looking through the passage and spotting the word or two which provide the answer. Correct answers thus do not demonstrate real comprehension – i.e. understanding – of the text, let alone any more sophisticated form of response, and it's therefore quite difficult to see what value such activity has, or what learning it achieves. Since such work is also such a drab and dull business, probably the most likely effect is to make children less willing to read more of the story, since reading *Alice* is apparently only an excuse to do boring exercises, and the text seems little more than a slightly disguised textbook. Even though this is rather an extreme case chosen to make the point, one can find essentially similar approaches in some of the brightly coloured modern English textbooks used in many classrooms in which the experience of reading even a really good story is inexorably followed by a set of dull and superficial questions, or other similar and equally. Such tedious and useless activities are cleverly mocked by Jan Needle in *Wagstaffe the Wind-Up Boy*:

> Have you noticed something about this chapter? All but seven of the paragraphs start with the word The, and all but nine with the phrase The Reason. This means that it is LITERATURE. Ask your teacher.

Perhaps just as common is the approach which involves using fiction as a 'springboard'[6] into some other aspect of the curriculum, a way of using a story as a means to a quite different end. Thus, for example, a book can be used not as an opportunity to develop response, but rather as a convenient way of enlivening historical or geographical topics or projects, or as a focus for artistic or technological work. The chapter in *The Turbulent Term of Tyke Tiler* in which Mr Merchant talks about the Normans is sometimes extracted and used as a source of quasi-historical evidence, or extracts from *The Midnight Fox* are used to support conservationist themes, and so on. Similarly, a variety of texts can be used as an opportunity to stimulate picture- or model-making, sometimes only tangentially related to the story. For example, I recently saw a wonderfully colourful classroom display of pictures and writing and models arising from 7-year-old children's work, following their reading of *Come Away From the Water Shirley*. It included pirate masks, mathematical work about pirate communications (flags, Morse code) writing about the history of real pirates, and all sorts of interesting and beautifully illustrated stories centred on imaginary piratical activities, all displayed under a huge skull and crossbones. I do not want to suggest that such work is no value as it is certainly likely that the children learnt a lot from doing it, and it is even possible that in the process children's responses to this delightful picture-book could have been extended and developed. But it is equally possible, and in this case I felt convinced, that the book had been used as a starting-point for all sorts of work which was essentially extraneous to the story, to the extent that the central theme, which is not really piracy but the power of Shirley's imagination to lift herself out of her humdrum everyday reality, was smothered and more or less forgotten.

One final point also needs to be reiterated. Powerful and genuine responses to stories are often, appropriately and necessarily, private. Many children occasionally, and some children frequently, do not wish to talk about the experience of a story; only the teacher can judge, in a particular case, whether it is best to try to draw the child out or leave well alone, but there are certainly times when the most significant responses are silent and tacit rather than explicit and articulated. Indeed, it has been argued that children's responses are like an iceberg, nine-tenths of which is submerged beneath the surface, or even like the Loch Ness monster – you think it's there and you hope to see it, but you're never absolutely certain that it really exists at all![7]

These issues do not need to be laboured. Rather we can return to the suggestion that the most important reason for reading fiction in the primary classroom is to extend and develop children's understanding and enjoyment of the story, and that one way of achieving such goals is by focusing on response. This means that children's activities following reading or hearing a story, whether planned or spontaneous, complex or unsophisticated, should have three characteristics:

- Activities should motivate children to read on, to read more, and to read more deeply.
- Activities should extend and develop children's understanding and enjoyment of the story.
- Activities should be closely related to the text, should draw the reader further in, not lead him away from it into different concerns, however valuable they may be in other contexts.

Language activities

Reading stories naturally leads to a wide range of activities which develop and extend children's linguistic and literary competences.

ORAL DISCUSSION

Probably the most valuable form of activity following reading is oral discussion. Reflecting on and talking about a story with other readers is, more than anything else, the most productive way of extending understanding. Sharing ideas and impressions and opinions of a book involves children, almost necessarily, in listening to and taking account of others' point of view, seeing a story in a different way, making clearer and more explicit their own views, and perhaps justifying their own opinion. In such ways children's comprehension, in the fullest sense, is increased. Such discussion activities also have the important effect of increasing children's motivation: to be part of a group talking about stories can enhance children's enjoyment and thus their enthusiasm to read more.

Such discussions do not always have to be organized in a very formal or structured way. Much valuable talk between teacher and child can be quite casual and brief, or sometimes quiet and personal, a natural consequence of sharing books together in the normal course of everyday classroom routines. If shared or group reading is organized in the classroom, as suggested earlier, children will often spontaneously talk about the story they have read. But in addition, some more systematic and regular form of discussion is likely to be worth while. For example, a class review of home and school reading may be occasionally useful, in which children are asked to say a little, even if only a sentence or two, about what they are currently reading, and their opinion of it. Rather more frequently, perhaps, organized small group discussions are valuable, provided that the teacher provides a helpful framework within which the discussion can take place.

Groups for discussion do need to be small, between four and six at the most, and – as with the shared reading groups discussed earlier – can be composed in a variety of ways from time to time, although friendship groups often work best. Initially at least, the discussion sessions should be quite brief: 3 or 4 minutes talk about a picture-book or a very short story is probably long enough, although the time can be extended to 10 or even 15 minutes if and when children become more skilled, and the experience is increasingly productive. It is often helpful to have a designated group leader to report back to the whole class, and a specified person to control the tape recorder if the discussion is being taped. If children are new to the conventions and etiquette of discussion, it is also necessary to make some rules explicit: the conventions involved are not ones that are natural to all children, but have to be learned. One class I visited recently had the following list of rules, devised by the children themselves, prominently displayed in their classroom:

Take turns to speak.
Don't speak when someone else is speaking.
Pay attention to what is happening in the group.
Don't distract other people.
Make sure everyone can see and listen.
No sulking in the group.
Only one person must speak at a time.
Don't be a nuisance in your group.
Don't disturb other groups.
Don't interrupt the group leader.[8]

As well as rules for discussion, clearly young children need help with the actual contents of discussion, with what sort of things it is appropriate to say and to talk about. For this purpose the concept of agendas is very useful: that is, the teacher provides the children with questions, suggestions or ideas which they are asked to discuss and then come to some conclusion. This is not to suggest a list of the kinds of closed questions which require only one-word – right or wrong – answers. Such questions are clearly not helpful in encouraging discussion, but tend to turn the whole experience into a kind of collective test. Rather the agenda needs to pose a variety of open topics or issues to think about, ideas to focus on, which can form a framework for discussion and help to prevent too much time being spent trying to decide what to talk about. Of course, as children get better at talking about books together, the necessity for a teacher-prepared agenda lessens; children may do without one altogether, or make up their own. But for inexperienced participants an agenda can usefully comprise questions which relate to the ways in which readers and text interact.

Generally speaking, like many other teachers, I have found it best when discussing stories with children to avoid most forms of 'why' questions (as in 'but *why* do you like it?') since most children find them very difficult to answer; to explain your reasons for a particular judgement is a very sophisticated skill. Better to provide questions which encourage children to talk about what they have read easily and without worrying too much at first about the depth of their perception. For example, if children have read the first chapter or two of a novel, they could be asked a small number of such questions as:

- *Picturing and imaging.* What has happened in the story so far? When and where did it happen? What pictures did you get in your mind when you were reading this? What did the story make you think of?
- *Anticipating and retrospecting.* What kind of story did you expect this to be? Have you read any other stories like this one? What caused this event to happen? What do you think will happen next? How do you think the story will end?
- *Interacting.* Could this story really happen? Does the story remind you of anything you've ever done, or other things you've read? How did you feel when this happened? How would you feel it happened to you?
- *Evaluating.* Which character did you like most? Do you know any real person like that? What part of the story so far did you like best? Were there any parts which were confusing or difficult to understand? Were there any parts which were funny or sad? Who was telling the story? Who do you think would like to read this story?

Of course, it's possible to go on to more complex or challenging questions if it's appropriate to do so: children can be asked to discuss their interpretation of the text they have read, justifying their responses logically by inference, deduction and reference to evidence within the story; they can be asked to consider the genre and the style in which a story is written, the implicit themes and ideas, the author's use of metaphor, imagery, irony and so on. In my experience it's not often necessary to do so because children begin to develop their own ideas about how best to talk about the story, but occasionally it may be valuable, especially with the more able readers who need a challenge. Certainly at first an agenda is often essential, and it's probably best to provide a small number of straightforward questions that enable children to describe, tell, or express an opinion and thus begin to explore their feelings and thoughts about the story.

An alternative approach is to give children occasionally a task to do which stimulates talk, rather than providing direct questions about the story to discuss. For example, groups of children could be asked to rearrange mixed and separated frames from a comic strip story into the correct order; to tell the story of a wordless picture-book; to look closely at the illustrations – front cover, accompanying text – in a story or novel, and to decide whether they add to or detract from the effect of the words alone; to try to tell the story from the point of view of a different character, such as the giant in *Jack and the Beanstalk*; to compare different versions of the same story; to devise questions to ask a character; to trace the development of a character through a story or a series; and so on. Many of these and similar activities are discussed in detail and in relation to specific books in the next chapter.

DRAMA

Drama, in all its range and variety, is another excellent way of extending children's understanding and enjoyment, since it always requires greater involvement in and with the story. For example, taking the part of a character enables children to empathize, to make connections with the thoughts, emotions, motives and actions of others in a very direct and powerful way. Similarly, improvising an existing scene from a story, or creating a context for a character beyond the story, requires making an imaginative leap from what is into what could be or what might have been.[9] Further, any kind of dramatization of a story is likely to entail the use of real and purposeful oral language, of making explicit in words what may only be implicit in the text. And adapting a passage of dialogue from a story, working through it with one's peers, involves looking hard at the text and making decisions about how the words on the page can best be translated into speech and action.

While for most children dramatizing a story is enjoyable and interesting and thus highly motivating; drama also provides experience of transferable skills: it necessitates collaboration in that children have to work together, talking, explaining, negotiating, practising, performing. These are valuable competences for all children, of course, but particularly for those for whom reading is often something of a lonely struggle. They too can participate more or less as equals.

Elaborate resources are not essential, but even the most simple costumes, masks or props, or the use of puppets, or an accompaniment by recorded sound effects or live percussion can add an extra dimension to a performance. Similarly, while plenty of physical space is an advantage, it's always possible to do something even in the most crowded classroom by using the space between desks, the aisles, the area at the front of the class by the blackboard, even the corridor. I once saw a performance of Maurice Sendak's *Where the Wild Things Are* by a class of 6-year-olds in which only Max moved around the classroom. The 'wild things' were confined to their desks, but managed to convey Sendak's fearsome yet somehow cuddly monsters with great exuberance. Thus, while it's possible, and very worthwhile, to develop a story into a sophisticated and polished production for a wider audience, small-scale and short-term dramatic activities within the classroom are just as useful.

WRITING

If caution is needed in using follow-up work of any kind, care is particularly needed in using writing activities. Generally, children find the various forms of oral response to story interesting and enjoyable, and thus are not likely to be dissuaded from reading. But this is more difficult in the case of using forms of written response: many children define writing of any kind as hard work – which of course it is – and are reluctant or resistant to doing more, with the additional potential effect of making reading itself less attractive. It could also be argued quite plausibly that on the whole children already do more than enough writing in the average upper primary classroom. For such reasons, if writing activities are to be used, it's most important that they genuinely fulfil the criteria of contributing to children's motivation to read, and their enjoyment and understanding of the story. Fortunately, there are a number of writing activities which are of interest and value. Most will be discussed in detail in the next chapter in the context of specific books, but some are of general relevance, and a brief mention of a few now may be helpful.

One of the most productive ideas is that children should keep a reading diary, or as the recent National Curriculum proposals put it, rather bluntly, 'pupils should keep records of their own reading'.[10] Ideally this should start as early in children's school careers as possible and continue all the way through school and hopefully beyond. Really, all that the diary needs to consist of is title, author and date of reading, but elaborations like a note that the book was or was not finished, or space for a word or two of comment, or a grading out of ten, or a 'star rating' for particularly good books, are also possible. Such a diary involves very little work for either teacher or child but builds up into a reading record which is interesting for the child and very useful for the teacher. Like many other readers, I have kept such a diary for many years now, and it's fascinating, if only to me, to see how my reading has changed and developed over the years from childhood, through student days, while teaching in schools, and on into my present job. It's also remarkable how often a title – *Anna Karenina* – reminds me of a time: July 1969, and a place – Crete, and a person – Lisa . . . what was her surname? – all associated with a particular reading experience which otherwise would probably be long forgotten. But the reading diary has more prosaic purposes for the teacher too: over the course of the school year she can use it to see whether and how a child's reading is developing, to discuss particular books with the child, to suggest possible new reading experiences, to encourage children to read a little more, or more widely, and to provide evidence for parents of children's reading. And if it is possible to arrange that in the next school year the new teacher continues with the same system, its value is correspondingly increased.

Writing letters should be for real, to communicate something to somebody, otherwise the activity is arid and meaningless. Learning how to lay out letters is important, but it is a means to an end, not an end in itself. Letters can be written describing or commenting on a favourite book and sent to friends in another class or school, perhaps as part of a wider exchange; Janet and Allan Ahlbergs' *The Jolly Postman* is a particularly valuable resource for such work, since the story centres on the theme of letters to and from different characters. Alternatively, children could write to the author – via the publishers – expressing appreciation of a book they have read, or questions about it. Most writers of children's books will respond with remarkable enthusiasm, although in fairness they should not be deluged with hundreds of letters. This is a particularly useful exercise, as well as being one that children find very exciting, because it helps them to realize that books do not just appear from nowhere but are written and illustrated by real, and ordinary, people just like the ones they know.

Writing stories is a very common primary school activity at all ages, and of course one that contributes to the development of children's literary skills.

The stories that children have read can make an interesting starting-point for such work. For example, children can make up their own stories about characters or situations that they have read about: what would happen if *Hugo O'Huge* came to your house, or visited your classroom? What story could you tell about your school after reading the children's accounts of theirs in *I'm Trying to Tell You*? What happened when Annie met the horseman from *Storm* again? This is a particularly valuable activity because children can learn something of the nature and problems of writing stories, and in particular the need for drafting and redrafting, without the need to rely solely on their own resources for plot or dialogue, since the original story provides a helpful starting-point. With younger children such stories can be constructed collectively and collaboratively and then transcribed on to the blackboard or into a large folder; or on to a computer word processor system. Children often take great delight in such collective stories, and they can provide a real sense of authorship.

Children's own illustrated stories can also be 'published'. With the increased availability in schools in recent years of microcomputers with word processing or even desktop publishing facilities, such ventures are quite easily managed, although hand or typewritten versions, which are then photocopied, are of course perfectly adequate. Alternatively, children's stories can form part of a class or school newspaper, or can be featured in a class 'radio programme' produced on tape. However produced, children's published stories can be a very helpful resource for the writer, who has at least one story that he or she can read confidently, as well as for other children in the class or in other classes.

Fiction across the curriculum

While the most obvious fiction-related activities are broadly located within the English curriculum, many others are feasible; for example, teachers can make productive use of stories in a wide range of subjects, notably history, geography and various forms of topic work. The possibilities are almost endless, but one or two examples will provide a flavour.

An activity which combines writing with the development of children's sense of geographical place is to draw and label a map or plan of the area of the story's action. For example, children can follow Finn and Derval in *Flight of the Doves* from England across the Irish Sea to their grandmother's home in Galway, or David's journey across Europe in *I Am David*, or they could trace the pioneer settlers in *Going West* across the USA. Closer to home, many stories, such as *The Turbulent Term of Tyke Tiler* and the *Church Mouse* series, provide a strong sense of physical location in streets and houses, or farms and fields, which similarly can be used to provide an interesting visual context for reading the story.

Illustrations are also valid forms of response to stories, and can take an almost infinite variety of forms. Recently, for example, on visits to schools I have seen a set of paintings arising from a reading of Oscar Wilde's perennial favourite *The Selfish Giant*, portraying the giant's garden at different times of the year; a whole-class collaboration on a huge picture of *The Iron Man* in white chalk on black sugar paper, which covered most of a wall in the school hall; a colourful mural by another class depicting some of the characters from *The Animals of Farthing Wood*; and a series of individual children's posters advertising the 'film of the book' of Charles Keeping's powerfully melodramatic version of Alfred Noyes' *The Highwayman*, complete with film stars' names, critics' opinions, performance times and so on. What all these forms of illustration had in common was that they arose naturally from the story and were being used by the teacher to enable the children to express a fuller response. In other words, creating pictures was a means by which the children could focus more closely on the story and thus understand and enjoy it more.

Conclusion

In this chapter I have suggested that:

- Readers, including children, interact with stories in a variety of complex ways; four of these have been described as picturing and imaging, anticipating and retrospecting, interacting, and evaluating.
- Teachers should encourage responses to reading by providing activities which increase children's understanding and enjoyment of what they read.
- Oral discussion is an essential means of developing response, and a basic constituent of classroom work with fiction.
- Appropriately used, other forms of language activity, such as drama and writing, can be valuable; children's experience of story can also be enhanced through classroom work in other areas of the curriculum.

It is time to discuss specific books in more detail, and to make some practical suggestions for using them.

References

1   The following discussion relies heavily on Benton, M. and Fox, G. *Teaching Literature 9–14*, Oxford, Oxford University Press, 1985.
2   Corcoran, B. 'Teachers creating readers', in Corcoran, B. and Evans, E. (eds.) *Readers, Texts, Teachers*, New Jersey, Boynton/Cook, 1987, p. 44.
3   Fry, D. *Children Talk About Books: Seeing Themselves as Readers*, Milton Keynes, Open University Press, 1985, p. 119.
4   Cairney, T. *Teaching Reading Comprehension*, Milton Keynes, Open University Press, 1990, p. 40–3.
5   Richards, H. *Junior English Revised*, London, Ginn, 1979, p. 159.
6   Protherough, R. *Developing Response to Fiction*, Milton Keynes, Open University Press, 1983, p. 11.
7   Fenwick, G. *Teaching Children's Literature in the Primary School*, London, David Fulton, 1990, p. 54.
8   My thanks to the teachers and children of Tamnamore Primary School, Dungannon, for this list.
9   An interesting recent example is Winston, J. 'Giants, good and bad: story and drama at the heart of the curriculum', *Education 3–13*, Vol. 22, no. 1, March 1994.
10 Schools Curriculum and Assessment Authority *English in the National Curriculum: Draft Proposals*, London, SCAA, 1994.

CHILDREN'S BOOKS

AHLBERG, JANET and ALLAN, *The Jolly Postman*, Heinemann.
ASHLEY, BERNARD, *I'm Trying to Tell You*, Puffin.
BRIGGS, RAYMOND, *The Snowman*, Puffin.
BURNINGHAM, JOHN, *Come Away From the Water Shirley*, Picture Lions.
BYARS, BETSY, *The Midnight Fox*, Puffin.
CARROLL, LEWIS, *Alice's Adventures in Wonderland*, Walker.
CROSSLEY-HOLLAND, KEVIN, *Storm*, Heinemann (Banana Books).
DANN, COLIN, *The Animals of Farthing Wood*, Mammoth.
HOLM, ANNE, *I Am David*, Puffin.
HUGHES, TED, *The Iron Man*, Faber.
HUTCHINS, PAT, *Rosie's Walk*, Puffin.
KEMP, GENE, *Charlie Lewis Plays for Time*, Puffin.
KEMP, GENE, *The Turbulent Term of Tyke Tiler*, Puffin.

MACKEN, WALTER, *Flight of the Doves*, Piccolo.

NEEDLE, J. *Wagstaffe the Wind-Up Boy*, Lions.

NOYES, ALFRED and KEEPING, CHARLES, *The Highwayman*, Oxford University Press.

OAKLEY, GRAHAM, *The Church Mouse*, Macmillan.

ORWELL, GEORGE, *Animal Farm*, Penguin.

SENDAK, MAURICE, *Where the Wild Things Are*, Puffin.

SEWELL, ANNA, *Black Beauty*, Armada.

SMITH, DODIE, *One Hundred and One Dalmatians*, Mammoth.

TRAYNOR, SHAUN, *Hugo O'Huge*, Poolbeg.

WADDELL, MARTIN and DUPASQUIER, PHILIPPE, *Going West*, Andersen.

WHITE, E. B. *Charlotte's Web*, Puffin.

WILDE, OSCAR, *Stories for Children*, Simon & Schuster.

6

Activities with Fiction

It's obviously not possible to discuss in detail more than a very small number of the tens of thousands of children's books available. However, few of the ideas and activities suggested are relevant and specific to only one story; most are transferable with a little thought and care to other similar books. Generally, the titles discussed are reasonably well known and easy to lay hands on; they are not necessarily the very best books ever, but clearly there is little point in discussing titles, however good, if they are not in print, fairly commonly found in libraries, schools and classrooms and thus accessible to teachers and children. Books go in and out of print at an alarming speed, but all those mentioned are currently available.

These ideas and suggestions are presented in outline form: to be utilized, expanded, developed, amended, or rejected as appropriate. For example, some activities are suitable for children while they are still reading the book, others are best left until it has been finished; some require a relatively high standard of reading ability, others are accessible to children of any level of attainment; some are suitable for a single lesson, others require longer periods of time; some are appropriate for individual work, others for pair, group or whole-class activity. Given the immense diversity of schools, classrooms, teachers and children, it's not sensible to attempt to provide definitive guidance in such matters, and so I cheerfully and optimistically leave them to the reader's discretion.

THE TURBULENT TERM OF TYKE TILER

GENE KEMP.
Illustrated by Carolyn Dinan.
Published by Faber (1977) and Puffin (1979).

The Turbulent Term of Tyke Tiler is popular with children in upper primary school classes because it is very funny but also rather sad at times; has a fast, exciting and gripping plot, and is written in the first person in an accessible language and style. The book is popular with teachers for these reasons too, but also because of the now-famous surprise at the end, and the opportunities this provides. It's probably best for children aged around 10 or 11. Page references are to the Puffin edition.

1 Agendas for group discussion can be constructed from any one of the many themes in the book. For example, there are several important relationships in the story: between Tyke and Mr Merchant, between Tyke and Chief Sir, between Danny and Tyke. Any of these can provide material for questions: How did Tyke find out about the teachers' plans for Danny to go to a different school? What did Tyke do to help Danny with the test? Was Tyke justified in what she did? Could Tyke have helped Danny in any other way? Why did Tyke confess to Mr Merchant that she had cheated? Or alternatively, children could consider Tyke and Danny's friendship: why does Danny need Tyke to be his friend? Why does Tyke remain friends with Danny, in spite of all that he does? Should you always do what your friend says? What makes a good friend?

2 Consider the question of Tyke's sex. Children often find the revelations of p. 119 quite startling! They could be asked to collect and present clues and hints from the book which indicate whether she is a boy or a girl. In fact there really isn't any evidence that 'she' is a boy: readers just assume that only a boy would be interested in climbing rockfalls, or would make friends with a child like Danny. And the pictures (e.g. pp. 40, 78) are ambiguous, despite what children claim. Second, there are some clues that she is a girl: (e.g. pp. 50, 89). Spud escapes housework as he is a boy but Tyke does not; 'unfair', says Tyke. She also has a developing relationship with her sister, and is fascinated in spite of herself with Beryl's interest in make-up and boyfriends (e.g. pp. 21–2, 90). This theme is obviously another that is ideal for a discussion agenda.

3 There are several action-packed scenes in the book which are particularly suitable for forms of improvised drama: when Danny lets Fatty the mouse loose in assembly (p. 28); Danny and Tyke at the leat (pp. 36–41). More ambitiously, children could improvise scenes that are not described but referred to, like Martin and Kevin 'tormenting' Danny when Tyke is ill (Ch. 13).

4 Many passages in the book lend themselves to preparation for reading aloud. For example, the opening scenes where Tyke talks to Danny about the £10 note (pp. 11–16), or that when Danny is discovered at the mill (pp. 106–14). Other passages could be prepared as dialogue alone, without a narrator, but perhaps with sound effects; for example the conversation between Tyke, Chief Sir and Danny (pp. 29–33), or Chief Sir, Mum and Tyke (pp. 98–100). A valuable extension of such work would be to make a tape of the reading for a specified audience (e.g. another class).

5 Children could be asked to look at the first sentence of the story – perhaps before the story is read, although this is not essential: 'We'd gone right through the school collecting the teachers' tea money and had got to the canteen door when Danny waved the ten-pound note at me'. What can we deduce about the kind of story this is going to be, just from these few words? Quite a lot, in fact. We can learn that this is a school story, set more or less in the present time, told in the first person singular, and that it includes, immediately, a mystery: where did Danny get the £10 note? In developing this activity it would be interesting to compare the directness and immediacy of the language and style with the contrasting opening sentences of one or two other stories; for example:

Mrs Frisby, the head of a family of field mice, lived in an underground house in the vegetable garden of a farmer named Mr Fitzgibbon.

(Robert O'Brien, *Mrs Frisby and the Rats of NIMH*, Puffin)

The Iron Man came to the top of the cliff.

(Ted Hughes, *The Iron Man*, Faber)

The island of Gont, a single mountain that lifts its peak a mile above the storm-racked Northeast Sea, is a land famous for wizards.

(Ursula Le Guin, *A Wizard of Earthsea*, Puffin)

From the Fosseway westward to Isca Dumnoniorum the road was simply a British trackway, broadened and roughly metalled, strengthened by corduroys of logs in the softest places, but otherwise unchanged from its old estate, as it wound among the hills, thrusting farther and farther into the wilderness.

(Rosemary Sutcliff, *The Eagle of the Ninth*, Puffin)

Such work of comparison and contrast could lead children to thinking about what the author of *The Turbulent Term* is trying to achieve in the first sentence. How does the sentence indicate what kind of story this is to be, and attempt to draw the reader into it? How successful is the author in intriguing the reader sufficiently to get him to want to read on?

6 Writing dialogue of various forms can be a worthwhile activity. Children could prepare a written (or oral) interview between a newspaper reporter and Mr Merchant in the scene where part of the school collapses (pp. 119–20): 'This is John Smith of BBC Radio Six. I'm in the playground of Cricklepit Combined school where a child appears to be up on the roof. Now tell me Mr Merchant . . .'. Another possibility is to base a dialogue on the conversation between Chief Sir and Mrs Somers about what should be done with Danny (pp. 72–3).

7 Chief Sir's comments are sometimes rather oblique, to say the least. Usually his words are explained (e.g. pp 30, 70) but sometimes they are not. What does Chief Sir really mean by 'I grow aweary of thy common sight' (p. 85)? If Mr Merchant's end of term reports included phrases like 'Tyke is a lively young lady' or 'Danny tries hard', what would he really be saying? 'She's a pain in the neck' or 'He can't cope with school work', perhaps?

8 Miss Honeywell says to Danny: 'Galahad's strength was as the strength of ten because his heart was pure. I think that's like you' (p. 87). A rather subtle compliment, but it makes Danny glow with pleasure. On the other hand, Mr Merchant's comments about King Arthur (p. 83) have the indirect effect of distressing Miss Honeywell. In other places compliments and insults are more direct ('Hooray for Sir', p. 44). Children could be asked to think of the power of words to make other people feel either happy or sad. No doubt they could easily come up with direct insults to Mrs Somers, but could they think of more subtle ways of describing her? Or compliments for Miss Honeywell, or praise for Dad on his election success?

9 The plot is quite complex, and groups could perhaps summarize themes and it sub-themes, although this is quite difficult, e.g. Mr Merchant and the history of the Normans; the election; the development of relationships between Mr Merchant, Miss Bonn and Miss Honeywell; or between Tyke and Chief Sir. Alternatively, it might be possible to identify turning-points in the story. The plot has certain crucial events, and pairs or groups of children could be asked to write a list of three

or four central moments: for example, a conversation is overheard by Tyke on pp. 72–3; Chief Sir believes Tyke on p. 114; Mrs Somers calls to Tyke on the roof on p. 119. Different groups' views of the most significant events could be compared.

10 Events and characters are related from Tyke's point of view (except pp. 120–4). How would other characters describe them? Children could write or tell Mrs Somers' description of Danny, Miss Honeywell's views of Mr Merchant, Martin Kneeshaw's opinion of Tyke. Or Danny could provide his account of his night alone in the mill (pp. 108–10) or Chief Sir could give his version of the mouse in assembly (p. 28).

11 Activities which focus on characterization are often interesting. For example: pupils could be given a list of opposites, such as noisy/quiet, clever/stupid, rude/polite, popular/unpopular, well/badly behaved, and could be asked to decide which fit each main character, and to justify their choices by reference to the text. Alternatively, children could construct a grid of co-ordinates, and then assess characteristics – kind, loyal, brave, honest, bossy, etc.– against the names of each character from the story. Or each child or group could be asked to adopt a different character and build up an illustrated dossier about him or her, as in a police file, e.g. name, sex, age, address, appearance, habits, family, likes/dislikes, typical activities, and so on.

12 Children could make a map of the area of the book's action. Obvious features include school, Tyke and Danny's homes, the leats, the mill, but also include the off-licence, the park, the Kneeshaws' house, etc.

13 As Tyke says, 'there can't be too many jokes' (p. 124). A class activity which always goes down well is to collect the jokes in the book and add lots more, for display in a class book, on the wall, or on tape.

SOME OTHER BOOKS BY THE SAME AUTHOR

Gowie Corby Plays Chicken, Faber, Puffin.
Charlie Lewis Plays for Time, Collins, Puffin.
Jason Bodger and the Priory Ghost, Faber, Puffin.
Juniper, Faber, Puffin.
Just Ferret, Faber, Puffin.
The Clock Tower Ghost, Faber, Puffin.
Dog Days and Cat Naps, Faber, Puffin.

GORILLA

ANTHONY BROWNE.
Published by Julia MacRae (1983) and Little Mammoth (1989).

Gorilla is a wonderful picture-book for older readers in the primary school. It's basically a very simple story, but Browne's imagination and brilliant technical skill take the reader into a surreal world where nothing is quite what it seems. Both adult and child readers need to keep their eyes wide open because there's a lot in the book that can easily be missed – even on the front cover. It's best used with children of 8 or 9 and over: younger readers can cope with the story but may not understand the quite sophisticated humour and wit.

1   This is a picture-book which almost demands to be shared and talked about. Much of such discussion tends to be natural and spontaneous as children discover the jokes – the light switch, the toy doll – and the references – the Statue of Liberty gorilla, Mona Lisa gorilla, Charlie Chaplin gorilla, John Wayne gorilla, Granny gorilla and so on; and investigate puzzles like the background to the picture of Hannah and the gorilla dancing on the lawn. But it's also possible to use more formal discussion to focus children's attention on the themes of the story. For example: Why was Hannah's Dad so busy? Why did Hannah throw the toy gorilla into a corner? What did Hannah think when she saw the huge gorilla? Why did Hannah think the orang-utan and chimpanzee were sad? Which are the most interesting pictures in the book, and why? What does the book say about whether animals should be kept in zoos?

2   Like many good picture-book artists, Browne uses the illustrations to extend and sometimes modify or even challenge the meanings carried by the text. An interesting activity is to ask children to try to say or write in words what the picture is saying. For example, there is a full-page view of Hannah watching her father who is working quite oblivious of her. We can't see Hannah's face but the posture of her body is nevertheless very eloquent: what is she thinking? Later in the book there is a double page with a small picture of an orang-utan on the left, and a wonderfully expressive picture of a chimpanzee on the right behind white bars, cleverly formed by the margins of the page. The words say: 'She thought they were beautiful. But sad.' What would the animals say if they could speak?

3   Another activity which involves looking and thinking is to compare and contrast related but different illustrations. For example, there are two pictures of mealtimes in the book. One is of Hannah and her father having breakfast, the other is of Hannah and the gorilla eating after they have seen the film. The pictures give very different impressions: one seems hard and almost clinical; the other soft and friendly. Children could be asked to think about how and why the pictures have such contrasting effects: for example, the cold blue and black colours, hard straight lines and sharp angular corners of the first, the warm red and yellow colours and soft round shapes of the second. Similarly, at the beginning of the book Hannah's unhappiness is represented by the picture of her in bed, in which the bars seem to constrain her just like the bars on the animals' cages later on in the story. This time the effect of the two pictures is rather similar: how do the pictures give such a powerful impression of sadness?

4   Children could be encouraged to prepare and deliver a short talk about this, or another favourite picture-book, to a group or to the class as a whole. Initially, such talks may last only thirty seconds or so, and indicate just the author and illustrator, the title, the main characters and the theme of the story, and a personal opinion of the book as a whole. With practice, children should be able to extend the duration and complexity of such talks. Obviously, it is not only the speaker who has skills to learn in this type of work; the audience too has to understand how to respond appropriately and constructively to each presentation.

5   Picture-books can lead naturally to picture-making of a wide variety of kinds, and it would certainly be possible for children collectively to draw or paint a collection of animals for a class picture of a zoo, or to construct a life-size picture of a gorilla. But perhaps more in keeping with the tone and style of the book would be illustrations which attempt to express feeling and emotion. For example, two pictures of myself, one in a happy cheerful context and another in a sad or miserable situation; or a picture of Hannah walking hand in hand with her father.

SOME OTHER BOOKS BY THE SAME AUTHOR

Piggybook, Julia MacRae, Little Mammoth.
A Walk in the Park, Hamish Hamilton, Picturemac.

Willy the Wimp, Julia MacRae, Little Mammoth.
Willy the Champ, Julia MacRae, Little Mammoth.
Bear Hunt, Hamish Hamilton, Hippo.
Bear Goes to Town, Hamish Hamilton, Red Fox.
Through the Magic Mirror, Hamish Hamilton, Picturemac.

THE THREE LITTLE PIGS

The activities suggested for *The Three Little Pigs* are of a different kind, as they relate not to one book or text, but to alternative versions of the same story, as follows:

'The story of the three little pigs',
in *The Fairy Tale Treasury*, edited by Virginia Haviland.
Illustrated by Raymond Briggs.
Published by Hamish Hamilton (1972) and Puffin (1974).

The True Story of the 3 Little Pigs by A. Wolf, by Jon Scieszka.
Illustrated by Lane Smith.
Published by Penguin Books USA (1989) and Puffin (1991).

'William's version', in *Nothing to Be Afraid Of*, by Jan Mark.
Illustrated by David Parkin.
Published by Viking Kestrel (1980) and Puffin (1982).

The best fairy-tales are intrinsic to the cultural heritage of a society. They are powerful and compelling because they deal with universal problems like good and evil, pain and death, and pervasive human preoccupations like love and marriage, family, and social relationships. Successive generations have heard them, enjoyed and learnt from them, and passed them on. But in the process of transmission, the storyteller has always made use of the stories for his or her own purposes: to comment on current conditions and issues, to point up the relevance of the theme to today. Thus, in the case of contemporary writers, ideas about the way we live and the relationships we have in modern society gain in power and accessibility by being expressed through the medium of the old familiar stories[1].

The story of the three little pigs in *The Fairy Tale Treasury* is traditional and familiar; this or any other standard version could be read to children first to remind them of the structure and outline of the story. This could be followed with *The True Story of the 3 Little Pigs*, which provides a witty and clever wolfs-eye-view of events. Finally, *William's version*, told largely in dialogue between William and his granny, is a delightful but sophisticated story in which the little boy explores his feelings about the new baby his mother is about to have; the interplay between the two characters, the theme of the fairy-tale, and the reader's knowledge and expectations is very subtle.

1   The comparison of the Haviland version with that of *The True Story* provides a fascinating opportunity for discussion centring on ideas about different points of view. Children could contrast what the traditional story tells us about why the wolf blew houses down - very little: the reader is left to infer that eating pigs is just in the nature of wolves – with the elaborate motives and justifications provided by the wolf in Scieszka's account. Alternatively, what are the different reasons given for putting the blame on either the wolf or the pigs? For example, that the wolf is rather easily frightened and outwitted by the third clever pig; or, in Scieszka's story, perhaps that the first pig 'wasn't too bright', that the third is a 'rude little porker', and so on. It's worth noticing also how, in Scieszka's version, the theme of different perspectives is deliberately introduced by the account of news reporters who 'jazzed up the story' because the wolf's version 'didn't sound very exciting'. This could lead to discussion of the ways in which even ordinary everyday events can be described in a variety of ways, and thus have different effects on the listener or reader: for example, children could consider antagonists' accounts of a playground squabble.

2   A classroom trial of the wolf could form an interesting and relevant conclusion to such discussions of motive and purpose, and provide a context for a dramatic retelling of the story. If some children can play out the main protagonists, a 'jury' of the rest of the class could be asked to decide whether, or to what extent, the wolf's story should be believed. 'Wolf's honour', he says after eating the second pig, claiming to have discovered him already dead: is the wolf's honour to be trusted? Is his claim that a pig is merely a 'ham dinner' for wolves in the same way that humans might regard a cheeseburger a reasonable argument? And what validity has his impassioned plea that 'I was framed'?

3   A simpler but equally effective alternative is to dramatize one of the versions: *The True Story* lends itself to lively improvisation, since the

outlines of the story are clear and full of action, whereas *William's version* is largely composed of dialogue and thus can be more appropriately prepared for reading aloud, with or without accompanying action.

4   *William's version* is a rather complex story; children often appreciate what is going on intuitively, but explaining it in words is actually quite difficult, and it may be that laborious interpretation is unhelpful. But one topic the story naturally leads to is discussion of children's own often ambivalent feelings about their siblings. Thus it may be useful to ask (providing children's family circumstances are sufficiently well known to the teacher) about attitudes to brothers and sisters, and reasons for likes and dislikes. Some children may have or be about to have babies in the family: how does the story relate to their feelings?

5   The three stories can provide models for the children's own creative writing. Younger or less confident writers may provide a story which sticks fairly closely to the traditional tale, but others might be able to write in ways which extend or develop one or more versions of the story. For example, what would the third pig's account be? What did the news reporters' 'jazzed up' newspaper article say? What happened when the wolf came out of jail? What did William – and what did granny – tell his mother when she got home from the clinic?

SOME OTHER VERSIONS OF THE STORY OF THE THREE LITTLE PIGS

BRADMAN, TONY, *Who's Afraid of the Big Bad Wolf?*, Methuen, Mammoth.
DAHL, ROALD, *Revolting Rhymes*, Cape, Puffin.
ROSS, TONY, *The Three Pigs*, Andersen, Red Fox.
TRIVIZAS, EUGENE, *The Three Little Wolves and the Big Bad Pig*, Heinemann.

THE UNICORN DREAM
DOUGLAS HILL.
Illustrated by D. S. Aldridge.
Published by Heinemann (Banana Books) (1992).

Some critics are rather dismissive of children's books published in series, on the grounds that books that are standardized in format and professionally packaged and marketed are unlikely to be of high quality. This seems a strange view; *Storm*, a story by Kevin Crossley-Holland, published in the Heinemann Superchamps series, has won the Carnegie Medal, the most prestigious award for children's literature, and many others are excellent. Series books have several advantages: they are short, entertaining, and accessible for children whose reading ability is not very high; they are often well written, sometimes by distinguished authors; a child who has read and liked one book in a series can easily recognize another that he or she will probably enjoy; and because they can be produced economically they are cheap to buy. *The Unicorn Dream* is a typically entertaining example, probably best for children aged around 7–9.

1   The nature of dreams is one topic raised by the story which can provide an interesting focus for discussion or written work. For example, children could be asked to describe a particularly vivid dream they have had, or to speculate on the bizarre forms the 'Dreamwhere' sometimes takes. A common belief is that dreams can foretell the future: is there any evidence that this works? When Brian wakes up and asks whether he is still dreaming, the unicorn replies: 'That's like asking someone if they're lying. This could be a dream in which I tell you you're not dreaming' (pp. 7–8). How is it possible to tell whether you are dreaming or not?

2   Unicorns appear, often as a symbol of purity, in classical myth and legend. More recently they can be found in the 1662 Prayer Book, in nursery rhymes, and in many stories, from Lewis Carroll's *Through the Looking Glass* (Puffin) to Richard Severy's *Unicorn Trap* (Julia MacRae). Children could in groups explore the history, appearance and character-istics of the unicorn: what it looks like, what it eats, where it lives, what it does, if and how it talks, and so on. This could be followed by similar investigations of other mythical or unusual creatures like the mermaid, the yeti, the dodo, the jabberwock (Carroll), or, more ambitiously, the hobbit (Tolkien), and children could summarize their findings in the form of a brief illustrated report.

3   The plot is a simple but very neat one, cleverly alternating between the real world and fantasy, and leading logically from the initial suspension of disbelief (p. 7), through the unicorn's problem ('a special bridge . . .',

p. 12) to its solution (pp. 34–5) and the satisfying fate of the Night-Hound (p. 40) at the end of the story. Children could, with some help, write a brief précis of the story which makes clear its structure, or construct a visual plan showing how the elements of the story link together.

SOME OTHER BOOKS BY THE SAME AUTHOR

How Jennifer (and Speckle) Saved the Earth, Heinemann (Banana).
The Moon Monsters, Heinemann (Banana).
Galactic Warlord (and series), Gollancz.
Goblin Party, Gollancz.

THE MIDNIGHT FOX

BETSY BYARS.
Illustrated by Gareth Floyd.
Published by Puffin (1976).

The Midnight Fox is a popular choice for teachers to read serially to children towards the end of key stage two and in the lower forms of secondary schools. The story is very well written and the occasional Americanisms (little league, strike out, and so on) do not detract from the enjoyment of the story; indeed they may provide opportunities for discussion of the varieties of English usage. The main theme of the book, the developing relationship between a boy and a fox, appeals strongly to many children of this age but what makes the story even more engaging and absorbing is that Tom, the child narrator, constantly makes funny, often self-deprecating, yet sharp and credible observations and asides about his own feelings and relationships and experiences. The following suggestions by no means exhaust the books' possibilities; several other writers[2] have usefully discussed its classroom use in detail.

1 Many of the chapters in the story provide interesting opportunities for discussion agendas. For example, after reading Chapter 1 children could be asked to consider the reasons why Tom's mother wants him to go to the farm, and why Tom doesn't. The argument between them can be explored, either orally or in writing, thus:

Mother's argument	*Tom's argument*
Tells Tom	I just don't like farms
Should try	Can't *try* to like things
Farm is lovely: animals	I hate animals
I want to go to Europe	Mrs Albergotti?
Threatens father: tears.	

The argument between Tom and his father can be discussed in a similar way, leading to the question of how and why Tom eventually says "All right, I *want* to go to the farm" and expresses the unlikely opinion that he always wanted a baby pig (p. 14). An opportunity for a similar discussion arises in Chapter 6 when both Hazeline and Mikey tell anecdotes to support their belief that foxes should be hunted, and children could consider what counter-arguments Tom might use.

2   Characters change and develop in the story, and so does the way both Tom and the reader respond to them. Children could look at the way Uncle Fred, Aunt Millie, Hazeline, or Tom himself are portrayed, by skimming through the story and writing brief notes about, for example, the physical appearance of the character, what impression he or she gives at first, and how this changes by the end, what are the most important things the character does in the story, and so on. For example, Uncle Fred is first described in detail on pp. 57–60: 'I still did not feel at ease with Uncle Fred. . . . We couldn't talk to each other'. His personality develops through pp. 75–80, 88–93, 94–9 and 104–6. By pp. 111–12, near the end, Tom and his Uncle have come to a mutual understanding: 'I knew that if there was one person in the world who understood me it was this man who had seemed such a stranger'. Similarly, Hazeline appears merely a comic figure on pp. 39–44 and 71–3, but by pp. 83–6 both Tom and the reader can't help feeling rather sorry for her.

3   Much of the humour in the book derives from the use Tom and Petie make of thinking and talking in headlines, occasionally (pp. 34, 54) also accompanied by a newspaper-style story. One of the skills children need is to be able to write in different styles, and the book naturally provides an opportunity to do so. After discussion of the characteristics of how newspapers report dramatic events (cf. p. 38) children could be asked to write the accompanying story to the headlines on pp. 46, 58, or 84.

Alternatively, children could consider what other scenes in the novel would make a good newspaper story (e.g. pp. 30–1, 96–9, or 108–10), and make up their own version complete with their own headline. Such work could even be extended into the construction of a full newspaper front page dealing with some of the events of the story, including interviews with participants, artists' sketches, relevant 'photographs', advertisements, etc.

4 The same theme of writing in different styles could be addressed by looking at the questionnaire Petie sends Tom (pp. 60–1). Children could discuss the form that questionnaires take, and the way the layout and punctuation is quite different from other conventional forms of writing. A questionnaire for Hazeline offers possibilities: How many meals do you eat in a day? (Two, three, more than three?) What do you eat for snacks between meals? (Biscuits, fruit, sweets?) What three foods do you like best of all? Alternatively, children could try to make a questionnaire for characters like Uncle Fred or Mikey, or even Tom himself, although these are a little more difficult to do.

5 The theme of the power of magic words is quite common in children's stories, but Tom's thoughts on pp. 81–2 illustrate their double-edged quality: being able to command others to act for you is fine, but what if they have the same power over you? Children could invent a magic word, and discuss how they would use it. They could also think about how Tom could have used *Tacooma* imaginatively (i.e. not just on Uncle Fred) to help the fox.

6 A further interesting theme for discussion is the way the illustrations in the book add to, or detract from, the power of the story. Having re-read pp. 36–8, children could consider the illustration on p. 37 and/or the front cover picture. Does the picture add anything to the description? Does it match the pictures in the reader's mind when reading the text? Does the colour of the front cover make it more effective than the black and white sketch? Which are the best or most interesting pictures in the book? Would the story be better without pictures at all? If appropriate after such a discussion, children could be asked to write a caption for some or all of the illustrations (*Attacked by cows!*, p. 55), or if they decide that the front cover is unattractive, they could design their own book

jackets complete with picture, blurb on back, title on spine, ISBN, and so on.

7 One of the attractive characteristics of Tom is his honest but amusingly exaggerated evaluations of himself as decidedly unheroic: he refers to his fears throughout the book (e.g. pp. 8–10, 17, 30, 58), and indeed at one point (p. 78) he describes the list of no less than 38 he presented to his parents. Children could list their own fears and compare them with those of a partner: are there any in common? To what extent are the fears realistic? Have the things that frighten us changed since we were younger? How can our fears be overcome? A chapter or two from Jill Tomlinson's *The Owl Who Was Afraid of the Dark* (Puffin) might be a useful follow-up read for such an activity.

8 Several passages in the story lend themselves to a dramatized reading. One of the best is the scene where Tom confronts Uncle Fred and Aunt Millie and confesses to letting the baby fox out (pp. 111–14), since it is a crucial moment in the story. After practising, children could make a tape recording of their reading, or present it live to other children in the class.

9 As usual with first-person narratives, the story does not tell us much of other characters' perspectives, except as interpreted through Tom. It's useful to ask children to think about different points of view in one or two scenes, and perhaps try to write another character's version of events, although this is not an easy thing to do. For example, what would Tom's mother say to his father when he came home from work (pp. 7–12)? How would Uncle Fred describe his confrontation with Tom on p. 112?

10 On pp. 121-2 Tom describes the way memories fade, and how he and Petie buried a time capsule. When they dug it up a year later they were surprised to find what they had put in it. Children could be asked to discuss or write a list and justify their choice of objects that they could put into their own time capsules to let the finder in several, perhaps many, years know what life was like for children in the 1990s. Such a project would be made much more exciting if it was possible to collect together some of the objects on their lists and display them in an appropriate container, or even actually bury them.

SOME OTHER BOOKS BY THE SAME AUTHOR

The Eighteenth Emergency, Bodley Head, Puffin.
Cracker Jackson, Bodley Head, Puffin.
The Burning Questions of Bingo Brown, Bodley Head, Puffin.
The TV Kid, Bodley Head, Puffin.
The Computer Nut, Bodley Head, Puffin.
The Cybil War, Bodley Head, Puffin.

BEOWULF

CHARLES KEEPING and KEVIN CROSSLEY-HOLLAND.
Published by Oxford University Press (1982 and 1987).

Like fairy tales, myths and legends are part of our cultural heritage, part of the intellectual furniture of members of our society, and all children need and deserve to hear and read them. They are also good stories; as Reyersbach has argued: 'The direct confrontation in the stories of basic human issues – birth and death, love and hate, courage and despair, good and evil – strikes an immediate chord in the imaginative world of the child.'[3] In one sense, then, *Beowulf* is a story of brutality and ruthlessness, but it is also one of heroism, fortitude and self-sacrifice. The language in this version is powerful and uncompromising, making few concessions to inexperienced readers, but it reads aloud superbly and the words are accompanied by magnificent monochromatic illustrations.

1   The precise meaning of words like myth and legend – not to mention folk-tale and fairy story – is often unclear to children. A brief but pertinent activity, therefore, would be to explore the similarities and differences between these terms, using any appropriate dictionary or encyclopaedia.

2   Similarly, attention could be drawn to some of the distinctive uses of language in the story, such as in the first two pages: the alliteration ('wept the salt-waves weeping'), repetition ('A story . . .'), metaphor and simile ('I'll fuel you') and unusual expressions ('cat-fire', 'six-stringer'). More simply, children could be asked to find and try to explain a few of the phrases or sentences which seem striking and original ('swilling stonecold mead'), or list some appropriate adjectives describing characters like Grendel or Beowulf. All such activities of looking at the way

language is used are valuable, but clearly there is a danger that such work can become mechanical and very tedious, and it would be a pity if it interfered with simply relishing the sound and effect of the story.

3   Beowulf faces three separate enemies in the course of the book, but in each case the structure of events is similar. Children could discuss or write down a list of the constituent elements of each adventure. For example, in each case there is a malignant and monstrous opponent, an attack on the hero or his followers, problems and obstacles – Unferth, useless sword, cowardly Geats – fierce combat, and rewards for the triumphant victor – valuable objects, an honourable death.

4   The intrepid deeds of Beowulf – for others, never for himself – could be compared by children in discussion with other examples of courage; Beowulf is physically fearless, but are there other kinds of hero or heroine? Can the children think of situations in which fighting is not actually the brave thing to do at all? An alternative activity would be to draw up a code of behaviour for Geat warriors and compare it with an equivalent modern code, such as explicit or implicit school rules, and discuss which is better. Such activities involve consideration of rather abstract and difficult issues, but perhaps the moral implications which children may pick up from the story (might is right, or if you don't like it whack it) need to be confronted in some way.

5   The events of the story are so dramatic that they lend themselves naturally to writing in newspaper headline and story format, as discussed in activity 3 relating to *The Midnight Fox*, on p. 114. In the same way, children could be asked to produce versions of pp. 17–22 or 25–37 of *Beowulf* in tabloid form.

6   The illustrations, particularly of the monsters (pp. 16, 20, 24), are powerful, even frightening, although, or perhaps because, they are not in colour. Children could be asked to draw a black and white illustration of their own to accompany an exciting event in the text, or alternatively to compose and illustrate an appropriate epitaph for the fallen hero.

SOME OTHER BOOKS BY THE SAME AUTHORS

K. Crossley-Holland:
Storm, Heinemann (Superchamps).
Sleeping Nanna, Orchard.

British Folk Tales, Orchard.

C. Keeping:
The Highwayman (Alfred Noyes), Oxford University Press.
The Lady of Shalott (Lord Tennyson), Oxford University Press.
Sammy Streetsinger, Oxford University Press.

A GIFT FROM WINKELSEA

HELEN CRESSWELL.
Illustrated by Janina Ede.
Published by Hodder & Stoughton (1969) and Puffin (1971).

A Gift from Winkelsea is a most attractive story for children of 7 or 8: it's short, easy to read, exciting and amusing. But there's more to it than that: the book is beautifully crafted. The descriptions of ordinary family life are so authentic that the intrusion of the mysterious Gift seems fascinating but entirely plausible. The developing relationship between the characters is cleverly portrayed, and the ending is perfect. Helen Cresswell is a prolific and popular writer, but this is one of her most vivid and original stories. Page references are to the Puffin edition.

1   The question of what the Gift actually is, never really answered in the book, fascinates and intrigues children, and provides a natural focus for discussion and often heated argument! In addition however, the story can naturally lead to discussion agendas. For example, 'All that for forty pence', says Mary at the end of the book (p. 73); what does she mean, and is she right? Why does Mary think that the Gift was 'the most magical and delightful thing that had ever happened to them' (p. 69)? How does Dan plan to replace the Gift, and why do you think Mrs Kane immediately says 'No!' (p. 74)? What are the arguments for and against sending the Gift to the zoo or to the PDSA (pp. 38, 62–3 and 68–9)? In what ways has the Gift's presence made the family different? What would the Gift say to the family, as he splashes his way up the canal to the sea, if he could talk?

2   The Gift's growth is phenomenal: 'he doubles up every day' (p. 33). Young children are not likely really to appreciate the dramatic effects of such growth, and interesting mathematical work could be done showing the results of doubling in size. For example, if the Gift first emerges

from an egg the size of a chicken's – say five centimetres long, to make the sums easier – and if he really does double in size every day, how long would it be before he is as tall as a child? And how long before he would be taller than the classroom? (The answer to both questions is less than a week.)

3   Chapter 6 – 'Aquarium Pet' – is one of several passages in the book which provides both a context and plenty of lively dialogue for dramatization. As Mary and Dan wheel the Gift along, they meet varied astonished passers-by, including a policeman, and then have to negotiate entry to the pet show with both the Vicar and the competition judge, before triumphantly achieving a prize as the most unusual pet. Such a dramatization could consist of a very simple reading of the dialogue, but much would be added by using a few simple props and costumes.

4   Children could be asked to find out something about Helen Cresswell, either a few very simple facts, or something a little more sophisticated. Examples of the former would be questions which can be answered by looking at the book itself, such as: when did Helen Cresswell write this story? Whom did she first write it for? Has she written any other books for children? Who drew the pictures in the book? An interesting extension of such a study could be stimulated by reading a brief account of Helen Cresswell and her work, such as that in the magazine *Books for Keeps* (No. 42, January 1987), or more recently in Michael Rosen and Jill Burridge's book *Treasure Islands*,[4] both of which also provide a useful lead into some of her other stories.

5   The final paragraph of the story (p. 74) provides a good opportunity for children to predict, either orally or in the form of a written story, what might happen if and when the Kane family visit Winkelsea again. Children's versions could then be compared with the book's actual sequel, *Whatever Happened in Winkelsea?*

6   In spite of the simplicity and brevity of the story, the vocabulary is quite extensive and challenging; there are many words that children may not know, but usually the context provides much assistance. Children could be asked to find phrases or sentences containing unknown words in one chapter perhaps, and then to try to work out the meanings before finally checking with a dictionary. For example, in Chapter 3: 'the Gift from Winkelsea doing its strange, *solitary* dance up there' (p. 26); 'At

that moment the egg, with a final *acrobatic* leap' (p. 27); 'you feeding it chips as if it was a *navvy* or something' (p. 29); 'and Mary just sat and watched, perfectly *rapt*' (p. 31). This is the kind of work which could easily become extremely tedious and detract from enjoyment of the story, but it might be valuable occasionally, if handled carefully.

7 The construction of a family album for the Kanes is an interesting activity, which necessarily focuses children's attention on important aspects of the story. An ordinary scrapbook is perfectly adequate for the purpose, and items can be added while the story is being read. The album can contain such features as pictures of the Kane's house and of the garden, including the tow-path and the canal, portraits of the adult and child characters and of the Gift at varying stages of development from egg to fully grown, the pet show entry form, the judge's competition notes, a 'blue rosette' (p. 55), a newspaper cutting (p. 71), children's diary entries at different points in the story, a letter to the local zoo asking for advice, and so on.

SOME OTHER BOOKS BY THE SAME AUTHOR

Whatever Happened in Winkelsea? Lutterworth, Puffin.
The Bongleweed, Faber, Puffin.
The Piemakers, Puffin.
Lizzie Dripping, Puffin.
Greedy Alice, Deutsch, Corgi.
Two Hoots, A.& C. Black, Young Lions (Jets).
Rosie and the Boredom Eater, Heinemann (Superchamps).

THE SELFISH GIANT

OSCAR WILDE.
Illustrated by Michael Foreman and Freire Wright
Published by Puffin (1982).

Also available in Wilde, O. *Stories for Children*, illustrated by P. J. Lynch, published by Simon & Schuster.

A famous story, written more than a hundred years ago, but not one to all adult readers' taste: it's a bit sentimental, and the religious imagery and allegory can seem rather cloying. But in my experience children of 7–9, or thereabouts, often enjoy it, and find it strangely compelling. It would be particularly inappropriate if a short story like this were smothered with activities, so one or two suggestions will suffice.

1   Children could consider and discuss some of the issues raised by the story. For example: what is selfishness, and what is the opposite? Why does the giant refuse to let the children play in the garden – and what does 'Trespassers Will Be Prosecuted' actually mean? What do the children do which encourages him to change his mind?

2   Children could also think about other actions or activities they have experienced which could be regarded as selfish or unselfish, or other stories which illustrate the same theme, such as the Good Samaritan (Luke's Gospel, Ch. 10) or, in a quite different way Aunt Sponge and Aunt Spiker in Roald Dahl's *James and the Giant Peach* (Puffin). Alternatively, a discussion of the characteristics of giants could be informed by the story of David and Goliath (I Samuel, Ch. 17) or Raymond Briggs' *Jim and the Beanstalk* (Puffin).

3   The story provides the opportunity for groups of children to draw or paint their own interpretations of the giant's garden at different times of year, particularly if they can do so before they have seen the published illustrations. If on a large enough scale, the resulting pictures could form an attractive display on the classroom wall. Alternatively, children could compare the illustrations in the two published versions (and they are very different) and suggest reasons for their preferences.

4   Dramatization of *The Selfish Giant* in groups of five or six children is not difficult since the story is short and coherent. It also contains a nice balance between dialogue and action. Children could rehearse their version and then perform it for the rest of the class.

SOME OTHER BOOKS BY THE SAME AUTHOR

The Fairy Stories, Gollancz.
The Young King and Other Stories, Longman.
The Happy Prince and Other Stories, Dent, Puffin.
Stories for Children, Simon & Schuster.

WAR BOY: A COUNTRY CHILDHOOD

MICHAEL FOREMAN.

Published by Pavilion (1989) and Puffin (1991).

There are a large number of excellent novels for children set in times of conflict, and especially centred on the Second World War (see Appendix 1, pp. 130–8). One or two such books, like *The Silver Sword* (Puffin), are among the most famous children's books written in recent times. However, perhaps because of the nature of the subject-matter, many of these titles tend to be quite challenging reads, which may be one good reason why *War Boy*, which is short, episodic, and fairly simply written, is likely to be more attractive for many children aged 8–10 or 11. Another reason is the illustrations; indeed, Michael Foreman is well known for his brilliant picture-books which often centre on social and environmental issues, and even more so for his distinctive illustrations for other writers' work, like Helen Piers' *Long Neck and Thunder Foot* (Puffin) and many others. And a third reason, most important of all, is that the book reads well, not only as a piece of social history, but also as a delightfully nostalgic story in its own right.

This book is also a good example of the fact that hardback is often much better than paperback, particularly in books with pictures. The Puffin version of *War Boy* is really of rather poor quality. The pages are only half-size, the original colour illustrations are in muddy shades of black and white, and many of the pictures are omitted, inverted, truncated, or otherwise mucked about. Better paperback than nothing, I suppose, but if money is available the hardback is much better value. Page references are to the Pavilion edition.

1   Discussion could focus on any one or two of the many events and adventures in the book. For example, why did 'No child set foot on the beach for the duration of the war' (p. 16)? Why was Miss Burgess so cross to find the children imitating Nazis in the classroom (p. 68)? And why did the author when delivering papers 'try to float silently over their crunching gravel' (p. 70)? Why did Michael Foreman go with the other children to pinch the Vicar's apples when, as he says, 'My mother had a shop full of apples'? And what does he mean when he says 'I should have paid more attention to the Lord's Prayer. And so should have the Vicar' (p. 83)?

2   Alternatively, children could be asked to think about questions relating
      to the book as a whole. For example, what are the similarities and differ-
      ences between children's lives then and now? Some of the differences
      are obvious – no television or cars, the relative poverty, the constant
      danger of bombing, the transient population of soldiers and sailors,
      corporal punishment in school, outside toilets, pillboxes, Anderson
      shelters, barrage balloons, and so on. Some children may also see more
      subtle differences: the powerful, implicit theme of the importance of
      family and community which runs throughout the story, the ever-present
      combination of sadness and jollity in the adults' lives (e.g. p. 33), the
      apparent independence of children (e.g. p. 22), the wistful tone of the
      writer looking back to days gone forever (e.g. p. 91).

3   Children could be asked to look for some of the striking images and
      phrases in the story, and to provide explanations. For example, 'her
      laughter stopped traffic' (p. 33), 'psychedelia came early' (p. 39), 'a
      chill would come from their letter-box' (p. 70), 'a golden citadel about
      to fall' (p. 78), 'dropping diamonds in the dark' (p. 80), and 'ominous as
      vultures' (p. 83).

4   Nicknames feature quite frequently in the story. Children could make a
      list of characters' real names and nicknames with possible explanations
      of the latter (e.g. Pud, Lofty, Squirt, Father Christmas, Pal) and then
      add others, either of friends or famous people.

5   The author was not at all impressed by his first visit to the cinema
      (p. 73), but the visual nature of the book makes it ideal for thinking
      about in terms of film. Children could, either individually or in groups,
      construct a poster for 'the film of the book', making it as realistic as
      possible, and including for example film-stars' names, critics' views,
      prices, performance times, etc.

6   The pictures in the book are so striking that they are worth looking at
      closely. Children could pick three or four which they like, which are of
      contrasting style, size, colour, medium or subject-matter, and then talk
      or write about what reasons they have for making particular choices,
      and/or try to describe how the pictures differ.

7   Having read the book and discussed aspects of its portrayal of wartime
      life, children could be asked to write an imaginative story about an

event or adventure which happened, or could have happened, to a war child, or perhaps a series of diary entries by a child of the time, using some of the characters, episodes or illustrations of the story as a stimulus. For example, a bomb coming through the roof (pp. 7–8); the pictures of the fire at the church (pp. 10–13); various ways of annoying old ladies (pp. 24, 26, 28, 40, 48); stories told by tramps and fishermen (pp. 60–2); an attack by raiders (pp. 52–4). The development of empathy is one important way in which children's historical understanding is developed, and this kind of activity makes some contribution, as well as extending children's understanding and enjoyment of the story.

SOME OTHER BOOKS BY THE SAME AUTHOR

War Game, Pavilion.
Dinosaurs and All That Rubbish, Hamish Hamilton, Puffin.
Panda's Puzzle and his Voyage of Discovery, Hamish Hamilton, Puffin.
War and Peas, Puffin.
All The King's Horses, Hamish Hamilton.
Trick a Tracker, Gollancz.
One World, Andersen, Red Fox.

BILL'S NEW FROCK

ANNE FINE.
Illustrated by Philippe Dupasquier.
Published by Methuen (1989) and Mammoth (1990).

Bill's New Frock is a wonderful example of a story which deals with an important issue in a way which is attractive and accessible to children as young as 7 or 8, but still enjoyable at ages 10 or 11; indeed the title alone is irresistible! Like much of Anne Fine's work for children, it's well written and very funny, but has a serious point to make. (Page references are to the Mammoth edition).

1   This is a book which naturally leads to discussion, not to say disagreement. There are three themes which seem particularly worth focusing on, and for which discussion agendas are easy to construct. The first, and the major theme that runs right through the book, is that Bill is treated differently because he is seen as a girl. Children could be asked

to list some of the occasions when this happens in the story, and then to consider why, and whether there are any valid reasons for doing so. In many cases children may think that Bill is treated unfairly, even when it works to Bill's advantage (e.g. pp. 12, 32), but, for example, is Mrs Collins really at fault for offering a 'Bunty' to Bill when there are very few comics left (p. 58)? In each case, how should Bill have been dealt with? The second theme is that of the dress itself, which provides much of the humour. What are the disadvantages of such a garment (e.g. Ch. 4), and are there any advantages (e.g. pp. 68–9)? To what extent are our perceptions of people affected by their clothes? Does it matter whether we come to school in scruffy old clothes, or neatly and tidily dressed, or in school uniform? And if so, why? Third, children could think about the issues raised by Chapter 6. If it is wrong to treat Bill differently because he is a girl, is it also wrong to behave differently towards Paul – by planning to let him win the race – because he is disabled?

2   Each chapter can be seen as a self-contained episode within the frame-work of the story as a whole, and each is told largely through dialogue. Thus different oral or dramatic versions are easy to organize. For example, groups of children could take a chapter each, and improvise the scene. Alternatively, one or more sections of the story could be written in dialogue and performed as a reading.

3   The story can be used as an interesting stimulus for writing. For example, children may be able to write an account of an occasion on which they felt they had been treated differently and/or unfairly because of their gender; or write out some of the arguments that could be used for or against girls joining in football in the playground, or lifting heavy objects (p. 14), or sitting at separate tables in the classroom; or imagine how their lives would change if they changed to or from being a boy; or their perceptions of the different ways they are treated by Mum and Dad, or by male and female teachers; or perhaps even write a set of rules for non-sexist behaviour in school.

4   Philippe Dupasquier's distinctive illustrations are worth a second look, and perhaps comparison with some of his other work, such as *Dear Daddy* . . . and *Our House on the Hill* (Puffin). Children could be asked to discuss the extent to which the pictures contribute to the humour of the story, and perhaps create their own illustrations, e.g.

of p. 12, the pink Bill on pp. 40–2, or the confrontation with Mean Malcolm, pp. 91-2.

SOME OTHER BOOKS BY THE SAME AUTHOR

Crummy Mummy and Me, Deutsch, Puffin.
Goggle-Eyes, Hamish Hamilton, Puffin.
Madame Doubtfire, Hamish Hamilton, Puffin.
Anneli the Art Hater, Mammoth.
The Worst Child I Ever Had, Hamish Hamilton, Puffin.
Stranger Danger?, Hamish Hamilton, Puffin.
A Pack of Liars, Hamish Hamilton, Puffin.
The Granny Project, Mammoth.

JOURNEY TO JO'BURG:
A SOUTH AFRICAN STORY

BEVERLEY NAIDOO.
Illustrated by Lisa Kopper (Lions edition only).
Published by Longman (1985) and Young Lions (1987).

If one of the functions of literature is to expand children's horizons beyond the here and now, stories set in other times and places have an obvious attraction, and *Journey to Jo'burg* is a good example of the genre. As Naledi and Tiro travel to find their mother, they explore the authentic experience of poor Black people living in South Africa, and the reader is skilfully drawn in too. But the book is not just a sort of fictionalized treatise on politics or sociology. The reader certainly learns a lot about a very different culture and society, but is also enabled to feel what it is like to enter into the experience; and thus the story exemplifies the way fiction can contribute to the development of empathy. It's probably best suited to readers aged 9–11, although older children may enjoy it too. Page references are to the Young Lions edition.[5]

1   A first brief activity might be to place the story geographically. A small map appears in the book (p. 9), but children could also look at an atlas to get a sense of the physical characteristics of South Africa, e.g. how enormous it is, and where it is in relation to other countries.

2   The story is located in a real time and place, and so some of the factual details in the book – most obviously the 'pass laws', pp. 17, 45–6 –

have recently, and happily, changed. However, the central theme of fairness and unfairness which runs right through the story remains very relevant and provides plenty of opportunities for discussion. Different groups of children could be asked to read a passage carefully (e.g. pp. 19–21, 38–41, 68–71), to consider the implications, and to contrast the experience of the children with their own. Some specific questions may stimulate such discussion; for example, when the children accompany Dineo to the hospital, why are there so many people waiting to see the doctor? Why is he so tired? What is the real cause of the young woman's baby's death? Why is Mma worried by what the doctor tells her?

3   Following discussion of one or more of the episodes in the story, children could be asked to write diary entries from the point of view of one of the characters; in other words, not so much a retelling of the story, but an account of perceptions and feelings about the events described. Children's individual work could then usefully be shared with others in the class, so helping to build up a sense of the emotion as well as the adventure of the story.

4   Again after careful reading of one or two passages, children could select a character such as Grace, Madam (pp. 39–40), the farmer (p. 21), the policeman (pp. 45–6), and then try to make up some penetrating questions to ask him or her. Then children could take it in turns to ask their questions, and to try to answer them in the role of the character. It's not always easy for children to move beyond questions requiring only factual recall of events in the book, but with practice it is possible for children to acquire some of the techniques and skills of the interviewer.

5   The story ends on a hopeful note, as Naledi thinks about the possibility of becoming a doctor, instead of a servant in a White family. Children could be asked to predict, orally or in writing, Naledi's future, before reading Beverley Naidoo's published sequel, *Chain of Fire*.

ANOTHER BOOK BY THE SAME AUTHOR

Chain of Fire, Collins, Lions.

CONCLUSION

There are, of course, dozens more good authors and hundreds more excellent books available for children to read and enjoy, some of which are listed in Appendix 1, pp. 130–8. There are, too, an almost infinite variety of possibilities and opportunities for using books with children in middle and upper primary classrooms; I hope that at least the reader's mind will have been stimulated by these few suggestions.

While I have been writing this book, two quotations have been at the forefront of my mind; together they seem to me to summarize much of what I have tried to say, and together they may, therefore, form an appropriate conclusion:

> reading means: cultural cross-referencing, contrasting of oppositional texts, resourcing alternative views, and making space in classrooms for the socialized interpretation of multiple meanings.[6]

> We are hoping to offer the world of literature to children; to show even the youngest, least mature beginner in books that within the covers of a loved book is an adventure of the spirit – something that can speak to that child alone and lead her or him into a wider world.[7]

In different ways, both writers make the same crucial point: it is the enthusiastic yet thoughtful interaction of child, teacher and text that creates, sustains and enhances the power of literacy. And as primary teachers it is our professional responsibility, more than anyone else's, to ensure that the interaction is constructive and productive.

References

1   See also John Stephens' discussion of the 'intertextuality' of children's books in his *Language and Ideology in Children's Fiction*, London, Longman, 1992, p. 84–119.
2   For example, in Thomas, R. and Perry, A. *Into Books: 101 Literature Activities for the Classroom*, Melbourne, Oxford University Press,1984; Bentley, D. and Reid, D. *Fiction Blue Set: Teachers' Resources*, Leamington Spa, Scholastic, 1993; Voller, J. *et al. Teaching a Novel: The Midnight Fox*, Coleraine, University of Ulster, 1985.
3   Reyersbach, A. 'Working with the ILEA's myths and legends pilot project', in Hoffman, M. *et al.* (eds.) *Children, Language and Literature*, Milton Keynes, Open University Press, 1982, p. 82.

4   Rosen, M. and Burridge, J. *Treasure Islands 2*, London, BBC, 1993.
5   See also Mirza, Shahana, ' "Journey to Jo'burg": reading a novel with years 7 and 8', in Evans, E. (ed.) *Reading Against Racism*, Buckingham, Open University Press, 1992.
6   Rosen, M. 'On the importance of books in schools', in *Books for Keeps*, no. 79, March 1993, p. 7.
7   Waterland, L. *Read With Me* (2nd edn), Stroud, Thimble Press, 1988, p. 41.

Appendix 1
Recommended Books

There are many different ways of arranging and grouping children's books: two recent examples are the six categories of the latest version of the National Curriculum requirements for English[1] and the twelve divisions of the excellent publication *Hooked on Books*[2] in which reviews of four forms of story – picture-books, short stories, books in series, and novels – are each divided into three types – easy, middling, and challenging. But perhaps the most obvious form of classification is by theme or genre: school stories, historical novels, fantasy, etc. On balance, this is probably the most useful approach for present purposes, since generally it is the topic of the story that most readily comes to the mind of both child and teacher reader. It is therefore adopted here – except for books in series, comic strips, folk- and fairy tales, picture-books, and short stories, which are listed separately – although two disadvantages of this strategy need to be recognized: many stories could quite logically be placed in several different categories, and two books centred on the same theme may be superficially similar but in much more important respects fundamentally different.

Any attempt to recommend children's books is necessarily rather ambitious because so many new children's books are published every year, each adding to the huge quantity of existing material. No selection can do more than provide a flavour of the range and variety, and quality, of what is available. As this list omits the classics of children's fiction – which hardly need further recommendation – and is also restricted to just a few titles for each topic, it is necessarily even more limited in scope. Further, of course, while the books suggested as far as possible meet the criteria discussed in Chapter 3, no two readers' assessment of the characteristics of a book are ever likely to coincide completely. This is in one sense part of the delight of reading at all, but it also causes problems for the compiler. Thus, for one reason or another, readers may well find that some of their favourite stories are missing; but I hope that both teachers and children will find at least some titles here of which they were not aware, and that they will be encouraged to explore even further.

References

1   School Curriculum and Assessment Authority *English in the National Curriculum: Draft Proposals*, London, SCAA, 1994.
2   *Hooked on Books: Children Reading Fiction*, London, Harcourt Brace Jovanovich, 1990.

Books in series

Antelopes, Hamish Hamilton (e.g. Sam McBratney, Sheila Lavelle, Catherine Storr).
Banana, Heinemann (e.g. Joan Aiken, Gene Kemp, Penelope Lively).
Blackie Bears, Blackie (e.g. Ann Pilling, Chris Powling, Martin Waddell).
Cartwheels, Hamish Hamilton (e.g. Adele Geras, Catherine Sefton, Dick King-Smith).
Gazelles, Hamish Hamilton (e.g. Beverly Cleary, Anne Fine, William Mayne).
Happy Families, Viking Kestrel, Puffin (Allan Ahlberg).
Jets, A. & C. Black, Young Lions (e.g. Helen Cresswell, Michael Morpurgo, Bob Wilson).
Ready, Steady, Read! Puffin (e.g. Martin Waddell, Shoo Rayner).
Superchamps, Heinemann (e.g. Robert Leeson, Mary Hoffman, Michael Rosen).
Young Lion Read Alone, Young Lions (e.g. Colin West, Karen Wallace).

Comic strips

Briggs, Raymond, *The Complete Father Christmas*, Puffin, *Gentleman Jim*, Hamish Hamilton, and *When the Wind Blows*, Hamish Hamilton, Penguin.
Dupasquier, Philippe, *Jack at Seat*, Andersen.
Goscinny, Rene and Uderzo, M., *Asterix* (series), Hodder & Stoughton.
Herge, *Tintin* (series), Methuen.
Higgs, Mike (ed.), *Dan Dare Pilot of the Future*, Hawk Books.

Hughes, Shirley, *Chips and Jessie* and *Another Helping of Chips*, Bodley Head, Young Lions.
Redmond, Diane and Kingsland, Robin, *The Comic Strip Odyssey*, Viking, Puffin.
Wilson, Bob, *Stanley Bagshaw* (series), Hamish Hamilton, Puffin.

Folk- and fairy tales

FAIRY TALES, TRADITIONAL AND MODERN

Ahlberg, Allan and Amstutz, André, *Ten in a Bed*, Viking Kestrel, Puffin.
Andersen, Hans Christian (ed. Lewis, N.), *The Snow Queen*, Puffin.
Briggs, Raymond, *Jim and the Beanstalk*, Hamish Hamilton, Puffin.
Browne, Anthony, *Hansel and Gretel*, Julia MacRae, Mammoth.
Carter, Angela, *Sleeping Beauty and Other Favourite Fairy Tales*, Gollancz.
Garner, Alan, *Alan Garner's Book of British Fairy Tales*, Collins.
Haviland, Virginia, *Fairy Tale Treasury*, Hamish Hamilton.
Jones, Terry, *Fairy Tales*, Pavilion, Puffin.
Rosen, Michael, *Hairy Tales and Nursery Crimes*, Young Lions.
Ross, Tony, *Goldilocks and the Three Bears* (series), Andersen.
Scieszka, John, *The Stinky Cheese Man and Other Fairly Stupid Tales*, Puffin.
Williams, Jay, *The Practical Princess and Other Liberating Fairy Tales*, Nelson, Hippo.

FOLK-TALES, MYTHS AND LEGENDS

Aardema, Verna, *Bringing the Rain to Kapiti Plain*, Macmillan.
Aiken, Joan, *The Kingdom Under the Sea and Other Stories*, Puffin.
Corbett, Pie (ed.), *Tales, Myths and Legends*, Scholastic.
Garner, Alan, *A Bag of Moonshine*, Lions.
Horowitz, Anthony, *The Kingfisher Book of Myths and Legends*, Kingfisher.
Jaffrey, Madhur, *Seasons of Splendour*, Pavilion, Puffin.
Keeping, Charles and Crossley-Holland, Kevin, *Beowulf*, Oxford University Press.
Kiri Te Kanawa, *Land of the Long White Cloud: Maori Myths, Tales and Legends*, Viking, Puffin.
Lewis, Naomi (ed.), *Cry Wolf and Other Aesop Fables*, Methuen.
Lines, Kathleen (ed.), *The Faber Book of Greek Legends*, Faber.

O'Brien, Edna, *Tales for the Telling: Irish Folk and Fairy Stories*, Pavilion, Puffin.

Sutcliff, Rosemary, *Dragon Slayer: the Story of Beowulf*, Red Fox.

Picture books

Ahlberg, Janet and Allan, *The Jolly Postman*, Heinemann, and *Peepo!*, Viking Kestrel, Puffin.

Briggs, Raymond, *Fungus the Bogeyman*, Hamish Hamilton, Puffin.

Browne, Anthony, *Gorilla*, Julia MacRae, Little Mammoth, *A Walk in the Park*, Hamish Hamilton, Macmillan, and *Piggybook*, Julia MacRae, Little Mammoth.

Cutler, Ivor, *Meal One*, Heinemann.

Daly, Niki, *Not So Fast, Songololo*, Puffin.

Flournoy, Valerie, *The Patchwork-Quilt*, Bodley Head, Puffin.

Foreman, Michael, *War and Peas*, Andersen, Puffin, and *Dinosaurs and All That Rubbish*, Hamish Hamilton, Puffin.

Hoffman, Mary, *Amazing Grace*, Frances Lincoln.

Oakley Graham, *The Church Mouse* (series), Macmillan.

Van Allsburg, Chris, *The Wreck of the Zephyr*, Andersen.

Varley, Susan, *Badger's Parting Gifts*, Andersen, Picture Lions.

Waddell, Martin, *Going West*, Andersen.

Wagner, Jenny, *John Brown, Rose and the Midnight Cat*, Viking, Puffin.

Short stories

STORIES BY VARIOUS AUTHORS

Ashley Bernard (ed.), *The Puffin Book of School Stories*, Viking, Puffin.

Colwell, Eileen (ed.), *Bad Boys*, Puffin.

Corrin, Sara and Stephen (eds.), *Stories for Eight Year Olds* (series), Faber, Puffin.

Eccleshare, Julia (ed.), *The Collins Book of Stories for Eight Year Olds* (series), Young Lions.

Fisk, Nicholas (ed.), *The Puffin Book of Science Fiction*, Viking, Puffin.

Hewett, Anita (ed.), *The Puffin Book of Animal Stories*, Puffin.

Hoffman, Mary (ed.), *Ip Dip Sky Blue*, Collins.

Ireson, Barbara (ed.), *In a Class of Their Own*, Heinemann.
Souter, Ian (ed.), *Stories to Read Aloud*, Scholastic.

STORIES BY ONE AUTHOR

Edwards, Dorothy, *The Magician Who Kept a Pub and Other Stories*, Armada.
Hughes, Ted, *How the Whale Became and Other Stories*, Faber.
Lively, Penelope, *Uninvited Ghosts*, Mammoth.
Mahy, Margaret, *The Downhill Crocodile Whizz and Other Stories*, Dent, Puffin.
Mark, Jan, *Nothing To Be Afraid Of*, Puffin.
Pearce, Philippa, *What the Neighbours Did and Other Stories*, Puffin.
Powling, Chris, *Daredevils or Scaredycats*, Lions.
Wilson, David H., *Elephants Don't Sit on Cars*, Piccolo.

Novels

ADVENTURES AND MYSTERIES

Ashley, Bernard, *Break in the Sun*, Oxford University Press, Puffin.
Bawden, Nina, *The White Horse Gang*, Gollancz, Puffin.
Cross, Gillian, *On the Edge*, Oxford University Press, Puffin.
Crossley-Holland, Kevin, *Storm*, Heinemann.
Leeson, Roberts, *The Third Class Genie* (series), Hamish Hamilton, Lions.
Lingard, Joan, *The Twelfth Day of July* (series), Hamish Hamilton, Puffin.
Macken, Walter, *Flight of the Doves*, Piccolo.
Mark, Jan, *Thunder and Lightnings* and *Handles*, Puffin.
Owen, Gareth, *The Final Test*, Lions.
Pilling Ann, *Henry's Leg*, Viking Kestrel.
Voight, Cynthia, *Homecoming* (series), Lions.

ANIMALS

Adams, Richard, *Watership Down*, Viking, Puffin.
Byars, Betsy, *The Midnight Fox*, Puffin.
Cookson, Catherine, *Joe and the Gladiator*, Doubleday, Corgi.
Dahl, Roald, *Fantastic Mr Fox*, Viking, Puffin.
Dann, Colin, *The Animals of Farthing Wood* (series), Heinemann, Mammoth.
King-Smith, Dick, *The Sheep-Pig*, Gollancz, Puffin.

McCaughren, Tom, *Run With The Wind* (series), Wolfhound, Puffin.
O'Brien, Robert C., *Mrs Frisby and the Rats of NIMH*, Gollancz, Puffin.
Thomson, David, *Danny Fox* (series), Puffin.
Tomlinson, Jill, *The Owl Who Was Afraid of the Dark*, Mammoth.
White, E. B., *Charlotte's Web*, Hamish Hamilton, Puffin.

FAMILY LIFE AND RELATIONSHIPS

Bawden Nina, *The Finding*, Heinemann, Puffin.
Blume, Judy, *The Pain and the Great One*, Heinemann, Piper.
Cleary, Beverly, *Dear Mr Henshaw*, Puffin.
Cresswell, Helen, *Absolute Zero* (series), Puffin.
Dahl, Roald, *Danny the Champion of the World*, Cape, Puffin.
Fine, Anne, *Madame Doubtfire*, Hamish Hamilton, Puffin, and *Goggle-Eyes*, Hamish Hamilton, Puffin.
Godden, Rumer, *The Diddakoi*, Piper.
King-Smith, Dick, *Friends and Brothers*, Mammoth.
Pearce, Phillippa, *The Battle of Bubble and Squeak*, Deutsch, Puffin.
Wilder, Laura Ingalls, *Little House in the Big Woods* (series), Mammoth.

FANTASY

Banks, Lynne Reid, *The Indian in the Cupboard* (series), Dent, Lions.
Carroll, Lewis, *Alice's Adventures in Wonderland*, Julia MacRae, Walker.
Cooper, Susan, *Over Sea, Under Stone* (series), Bodley Head, Puffin.
Cresswell, Helen, *A Gift from Winklesea*, Puffin.
Hinton, Nigel, *Beaver Towers*, Knight.
King, Clive, *Stig of the Dump*, Viking Kestrel, Puffin.
Lewis, C. S., *The Magician's Nephew* (series), Collins, Lions.
Norton, Mary, *The Borrowers* (series), Puffin.
Pearce, Philippa, *Tom's Midnight Garden*, Oxford University Press, Puffin.
Pratchett, Terry, *Truckers* (series), Doubleday, Corgi.
Sleigh, Barbara, *Carbonel* (series), Puffin.
Storr, Catherine, *Marianne Dreams*, Lutterworth, Puffin.

GHOSTS AND MAGIC

Arkle, Phyllis, *Magic at Midnight*, Puffin.
Chambers, Aidan, *Ghost After Ghost*, Puffin.

Garfield, Leon, *The Ghost Downstairs*, Puffin.
Garner, Alan, *Elidor*, Collins, Lions.
Jones, Diana Wynne, *Charmed Life* (series), Mammoth.
Kemp, Gene, *The Clock Tower Ghost*, Puffin.
Lively, Penelope, *The Ghost of Thomas Kempe*, Mammoth.
Sefton, Catherine, *The Ghost and Bertie Boggin*, Puffin.
Swindells, Robert, *Room 13*, Doubleday, Yearling.

GIANTS, WITCHES, ETC.

Barry, Margaret Stuart, *Simon and the Witch* (series), Young Lions.
Dahl, Roald, *The BFG*, Cape, Puffin.
Gordon, John, *The Giant Under The Snow*, Hutchinson, Puffin.
Hughes, Ted, *The Iron Man* and *The Iron Woman*, Faber.
Manning, Rosemary, *Green Smoke* (series), Puffin.
Matthews, Andrew, *Wickedoz* (series) Mammoth.
Murphy, Jill, *The Worst Witch* (series), Viking, Puffin.
Tolkien, J.R.R., *The Hobbit*, Unwin.
Traynor, Shaun, *Hugo O'Huge* and *The Giants' Olympics*, Poolbeg.
Wilde, Oscar, *Stories for Children*, Simon & Schuster.

HISTORICAL

Aiken, Joan, *The Wolves of Willoughby Chase* (series), Cape, Red Fox.
Anderson, Rachel, *Paper Faces*, Oxford University Press, Lions.
Conlon-McKenna, Marita, *Under the Hawthorn Tree*, Viking, Puffin.
Cresswell, Helen, *The Piemakers*, Puffin.
Doherty, Berlie, *Granny Was a Buffer Girl*, Heinemann, Lions.
Garfield, Leon, *Smith*, Puffin.
Garner, Alan, *The Stone Book Quartet*, Collins.
Harnett, Cynthia, *The Woolpack*, Puffin.
Stevens, Carol, *Anna, Grandpa and the Big Storm*, Puffin.
Sutcliffe, Rosemary, *The Eagle of the Ninth*, Puffin.
Walsh, Jlll Paton, *The Butty Boy*, Puffin.

HUMOUR

Brown, Jeff, *Flat Stanley*, Methuen, Mammoth.
Cleary, Beverly, *Ramona the Pest* (series), Hamish Hamilton, Puffin.

Coren, Alan, *Lone Arthur* (series), Robson.
Hawkins, Colin and Jacqui, *Spooks* (series), Picture Lions.
Juster, Norton, *The Phantom Tollbooth*, Lions.
Lavelle, Sheila, *My Best Fiend* (series), Young Lions.
Mahy, Margaret, *The Great Piratical Rumbustification*, Puffin.
Ryan, Margaret, *Queen Bea the Champion* (series), Mammoth.
Wilson, Bob, *Ging Gang Goolie It's an Alien*, Young Lions.
Wilson, Forrest, *Super Gran* (series), Puffin.

MULTICULTURAL

Appiah, Peggy, *Tales of an Ashanti Father*, Deutsch.
Armstrong, William, *Sounder*, Puffin.
Berry, James, *A Thief in the Village and Other Stories*, Hamish Hamilton, Puffin.
Bond, Ruskin, *Flames in the Forest* (series), Puffin.
Cameron Ann, *The Julian Stories* (series), Gollancz, Young Lions.
Charles, Faustin, *Under the Storyteller's Spell: Folk Tales from the Caribbean*, Puffin.
Desai, Anita, *The Village by the Sea: An Indian Family Story*, Heinemann, Puffin.
Gavin, Jamila, *The Magic Orange Tree*, Mammoth.
Hallworth, Grace, *Mouth Open, Story Jump Out*, Mammoth.
Naidoo, Beverley, *Journey to Jo 'burg: A South African Story*, Longman, Young Lions.
Needle, Jan, *My Mate Shofiq*, Collins, Lions.

SCHOOL

Ashley, Bernard, *I'm Trying To Tell You*, Puffin, *Dinner Ladies Don't Count*, Julia MacRae, Puffin, and *The Trouble With Donovan Croft*, Puffin.
Byars, Betsy, *The Eighteenth Emergency*, Bodley Head, Puffin.
Carpenter, Humphrey, *Mr Majeika* (series), Viking Kestrel, Puffin.
Cross, Gillian, *The Demon Headmaster* and *The Prime Minister's Brain*, Oxford University Press, Puffin.
De Jong, Meindert, *The Wheel on the School*, Puffin.
Fine, Anne, *Bill's New Frock*, Methuen, Mammoth.
Kemp, Gene, *The Turbulent Term of Tyke Tiler* (series), Collins, Puffin.
McBratney, Sam, *Zesty* (series), Hamish Hamilton.

Mark, Jan, *Hairs in the Palm of Your Hand*, Viking, Puffin.
Rosen, Michael, *The Class Two Monster*, Heinemann.

SCIENCE FICTION

Christopher, John, *The Prince in Waiting* (series), Collins.
Curtis, Philip, *Mr Browser and the Brain Sharpeners* (series), Andersen, Puffin.
Dickinson, Peter, *The Devil's Children* (series), Puffin.
Fisk, Nicholas, *Trillions*, Macmillan, Puffin, and *Grinny*, Collins, Puffin.
Hill, Douglas, *The Moon Monsters* and *The Unicorn Dream*, Heinemann.
Hoover, H.M., *Children of Morrow*, Puffin.
Le Guin, Ursula, *A Wizard of Earthsea* (series), Gollancz, Puffin.
L'Engle, Madeleine, *A Wrinkle in Time*, Puffin.
Mayne, William, *Skiffy*, Puffin.

WAR

Bawden, Nina, *Carrie's War*, Gollancz, Puffin.
Davies, Andrew, *Conrad's War*, Heinemann, Hippo.
Foreman, Michael, *War Boy: a Country Childhood*, Pavilion, Puffin, and *War Game*, Pavilion.
Holm, Anne, *I Am David*, Methuen, Mammoth.
Kerr, Judith, *When Hitler Stole Pink Rabbit*, Collins, Lions.
Magorian, Michelle, *Goodnight Mr Tom*, Puffin.
Rees, David, *The Exeter Blitz*, Heinemann.
Richter, Hans Peter, *Friedrich*, Heinemann, Puffin.
Serraillier, Ian, *The Silver Sword*, Heinemann, Puffin.
Westall, Robert, *The Machine Gunners*, Nelson, Puffin, and *The Kingdom by the Sea*, Heinemann, Mammoth.

Appendix 2
Resources

Reading and Language Information Centre, University of Reading, Bulmershe Court, Earley, Reading, RG6 lHY.
Centre for Language in Primary Education, Webber Row Teachers' Centre, Webber Row, London SE1 8QW.

ASSOCIATIONS

National Association for the Teaching of English, Broadfield Business Centre, 50 Broadfield Road, Sheffield, S8 OXJ.
School Library Association, Liden Library, Barrington Close, Liden, Swindon, SN3 6HF.
The Book Trust, Book House, 45 East Hill, London SW18 2QZ.
United Kingdom Reading Association, c/o Edge Hill College of Higher Education, St Helen's Road, Ormskirk, Lancs.
Youth Libraries Group, Remploy, London Road, Newcastle under Lyme, ST5 lRX.
School Bookshop Association, 6 Brightfield Road, Lee, London SE12 8QF.

JOURNALS AND MAGAZINES

The School Librarian, School Library Association, Liden Library, Barrington Close, Liden, Swindon, SN3 6HF.
Books for Keeps, 6 Brightfield Road, Lee, London SE12 8QF.
Signal, Thimble Press, Lockwood, Station Road, Woodchester, Stroud, GL5 SEQ.
Children's Literature in Education, IBIS Information Services Ltd, Waterside Lowbell Lane, Colney, St Albans, AL2 lDX.

CHILDREN'S BOOK CLUBS

Books for Children, PO Box 70, Cirencester, Glos., GL7 7BR.
Letterbox Library, Unit 2D, Leroy House, 436 Essex Road, London N1 3QP.
Puffin Book Club, 27 Wright's Lane, London W8 5BR.
Red House Book Club, The Red House, Witney, Oxfordshire, OX8 5YF.
Scholastic Book Clubs, Westfield Road, Southam, Leamington Spa, CV33 OBR.

CHILDREN'S BOOK COLLECTIONS

Kaleidoscope, Books for Students, Bird Road, Heathcote, Warwickshire, CV34 6TB.
Kaleidoscope's collection draws on books from a variety of publishers. Other collections consist only or mainly of books from one publisher: such as Book Bus (Collins), Puffin Library Bookshelves (Oliver & Boyd), Picturemacs Pack (Macmillan).

VIDEOS AND AUDIOTAPES

Authorbank Videos, The Book Trust, Book House, 45 East Hill, London SW18 2QZ.
Weston Woods, 14 Friday Street, Henley on Thames, Oxfordshire, RG9 1AH.
Cover to Cover Audiotapes (Puffin).
Listening and Reading Audiotapes (BBC/Longman).

Bibliography

This is nothing like an exhaustive list, but merely a few of the books about children's fiction and related issues that are particularly interesting and useful.

APPLEBEE, A. *The Child's Concept of Story*, Chicago, University of Chicago Press, 1978.

BEARD, R. (ed.) *Teaching Literacy, Balancing Perspectives*, Sevenoaks, Hodder & Stoughton, 1993.

BENTLEY, D. *et al. Inspirations for the Independent Reader*, Leamington Spa, Scholastic, 1992.

BENTON, M. and FOX, G. *Teaching Literature Nine to Fourteen*, Oxford University Press, 1985.

BRANSTON, P. and PROVIS, M. *Children and Parents Enjoying Reading*, London, Hodder & Stoughton, 1986.

CAIRNEY, T. H. *Teaching Reading Comprehension*, Milton Keynes, Open University Press, 1990.

CAMPBELL, R. *Reading Real Books*, Milton Keynes, Open University Press, 1992.

CHAMBERS, A. *The Reading Environment*, Stroud, Thimble Press, 1991.

EGOFF, S. *et al.* (eds.) *Only Connect: Readings on Children's Literature*, Oxford, Oxford University Press, 1980.

FENWICK, G. *Teaching Children's Literature in the Primary School*, London, David Fulton, 1990.

FRY, D. *Children Talk About Books: Seeing Themselves as Readers*, Milton Keynes, Open University Press, 1985.

GAWITH, G. *Library Alive!*, London, A. & C. Black, 1987.

HOBSON, M. MADDEN, J. and PRYTHERCH, R. *Children's Fiction Sourcebook*, Aldershot, Ashgate, 1991.

Hooked on Books: Children Reading Fiction, London, Harcourt Brace Jovanovich, 1990.

HOWE, A. and JOHNSON, J. *Common Bonds: Storytelling in the Classroom*, London, Hodder and Stoughton, 1992.

HUNT, P (ed.) *Children's Literature: the Development of Criticism*, London, Routledge, 1990.

Bibliography

HUNT, P (ed.) *Literature for Children: Contemporary Criticism*, London, Routledge, 1992.

LANDSBERG, M. *The World of Children's Books*, London, Simon & Schuster, 1988.

LEESON, R. *Reading and Righting*, London, Collins, 1985.

MARRIOTT, S. *Picture Books in the Primary Classroom*, London, Paul Chapman, 1991.

MEEK, M. *On Being Literate*, London, Bodley Head, 1991.

MEEK, M. *How Texts Teach What Children Learn*, Stroud, Thimble Press, 1988.

MEEK, M. *et al.* (eds.) *The Cool Web: The Pattern of Children's Reading*, London, Bodley Head, 1977.

MEEK, M. and MILLS, C. (eds.) *Language and Literacy in the Primary School*, Lewes, Falmer Press, 1988.

MOON, C. and RABAN, B. *A Question of Reading*, London, David Fulton, 1992.

PINSENT, P. (ed.) *The Power of the Page: Children's Books and their Readers*, London, David Fulton, 1993.

PROTHEROUGH, R. *Developing Response to Fiction*, Milton Keynes, Open University Press, 1983.

ROSEN, B. *And None of It Was Nonsense: The Power of Storytelling in School*, London, Mary Glasgow, 1988.

ROSEN, M. and BURRIDGE, J. *Treasure Islands 2*, London, BBC, 1993.

SHORT, H. *Bright Ideas: Using Books in the Classroom*, Leamington Spa, Scholastic, 1989.

SPINK, J. *Children as Readers*, London, Clive Bingley, 1989.

STEPHENS, J. *Language and Ideology in Children's Fiction*, London, Longman, 1992.

STYLES, M. *et al.* (eds.) *After Alice: Exploring Children's Literature*, London, Cassell, 1992.

THOMAS, R. and PERRY, A. *Into Books: 101 Literature Activities for the Classroom*, Melbourne, Oxford University Press, 1984.

THORPE, D. *Reading for Fun*, Cranfield, Cranfield Press, 1988.

TOWNSEND, J. *Written for Children* (3rd edn), Harmondsworth, Penguin, 1987.

TRELEASE, J. *The Read-Aloud Handbook*, Harmondsworth, Penguin, 1984.

TUCKER, N. *The Child and the Book: A Psychological and Literary Exploration*, Cambridge, Cambridge University Press, 1981.

WADE, B. (ed.) *Reading for Real*, Milton Keynes, Open University Press, 1990.

WEIR, L. *Telling the Tale: a Storytelling Guide*, Youth Libraries Group, 1988.

WELLS, G. *The Meaning Makers: Children Learning Language and Using Language to Learn*, London, Hodder & Stoughton, 1987.

Index